WAITING ON YOUR PROMISE

≡ ❖ ≡

TARA A. BLACK

authorHOUSE™

1663 LIBERTY DRIVE, SUITE 200
BLOOMINGTON, INDIANA 47403
(800) 839-8640
WWW.AUTHORHOUSE.COM

AuthorHouse™
1663 Liberty Drive, Suite 200
Bloomington, IN 47403
www.authorhouse.com
Phone: 1-800-839-8640

AuthorHouse™ UK Ltd.
500 Avebury Boulevard
Central Milton Keynes, MK9 2BE
www.authorhouse.co.uk
Phone: 08001974150

First published by AuthorHouse 2/6/2006

ISBN: 1-4208-9532-X (sc)

Printed in the United States of America
Bloomington, Indiana

This book is printed on acid-free paper.

ACKNOWLEDGMENTS

I would be amiss if I did not take a moment to acknowledge all those who have been of the utmost support to me. First and foremost, I give all glory and honor to God for his guidance and for choosing me to be the vessel or vehicle to speak to his people.

There were a number of people who have been very supportive and assisted me during this process. I could never name everyone, but I pray that God will tremendously bless each of you for your continued prayers, editing and encouragement. There were some who had to read this a much as me and then there were the ones who made sure I stayed on top of it and were my motivation like my mother, Althea Black and my Pastor, Rev. Dr. Patricia A. Phillips who saw the book in the making.

All the illustrations were created by W. Troy Henley. I had the opportunity to meet him in the past few years and he willingly offered his time to help me anyway he could.

Again, I thank God for all those people he has brought into my life and who has been a blessing throughout my life. I thank God for my family and my wonderful son. I praise God for what he is doing in my life and what he will do through yours as you read this book and apply God's principles to your lives.

FOREWARD

I want to thank Ms. Black for being obedient to the spirit of the Lord in writing this book. It has been a blessing to me since its inception. What nuggets of truth have fallen from this book that I have enjoyed reading each chapter as they were completed. This book has answered some of the questions I have had in my own life, in dealing with my own circumstances. This book has revealed to me the strategic steps necessary to overcome obstacles in the single walk, while I am at this stage. It has reaffirmed the promise of a life that includes a mate, it has renewed hope and anticipation that seemed as though it had retreated and died. Waiting on your Promise is what I think other singles need to read in order to have them refocus on God. To work for his good pleasure, this takes our minds off of the world's agenda, timetable and quiets our own inner voices. I look forward to forgetting the past so that I may move towards the future. This book has challenged me to say again, 'use me Lord for your service', renew my commitment to him for then he can show me what he has been working on during the time my eyes were on him and not my past or current state.

So, I urge everyone especially singles to read and mediate on the words in this book and allow the spirit to minister, heal, renew and direct.

Sylvia McCray

CONTENTS

CHAPTER 4

CHAPTER 5

CHAPTER 6

INTRODUCTION

___*Waiting for Your Promise*___ was birthed from a seminar called "Saved, Sanctified, Single Woman" geared towards the struggles of the single woman. Sometimes, it feels like no one else is going through or struggling as much as your own self. Especially as a Christian, we often feel like we should not have certain feelings about our singleness and that we should not struggle with it. After all, Paul said that he learned to be content in whatever state he was in. However, I believe Paul had to get to that place of contentment in every aspect of his life. That is why he said he learned. Through time and growth, we learn to handle life's situations as they come. However, at times, we all need to hear of someone else who went through their various tests and trials. We need to hear how our fellow sisters make it through the lonely nights and that we are not alone in our daily struggles. As I had opportunity to talk with other single women, I found that we all have our set of issues, concerns and frustrations. However, the commonality of us all is the feeling that we are in it alone and no one else is going through. People just seem to live their lives but what you see is not always a true glimpse of what is happening since we have learned how to camouflage and cover our inadequacies. However, just to know that we are not alone in itself can be comforting. But knowing how to make it to the next level is even better. Keep in mind that this book is not a step-by-step manual to get a man. It is not a full proof plan that teaches women how men think. But rather, it is a process manual by which you might be encouraged to wait on God's perfect timing for your life.

As we go throughout our lives, we are faced with many decisions, obstacles, test and trials. We will endure the best of times as well as the hardest of times. Many relationships are established. At the same time, many dissolve as people and their ideas, opinions and desires change. While in our minds, we often wonder does it all have a meaning, what is its purpose or why it happened. Of course, no one ever questions the good. Many people go through life trying to find their real purpose. Many people go through life struggling to find themselves and to fill that void that we all feel at some point or another. Eventually, we are confronted by that image in the mirror that people see but they really do not know the depth of the emptiness felt within. Yet, He knows the depths of our hearts and is waiting to fill those empty spaces.

God has so plotted and preordained that each of us can come to know him in a way no one could ever imagine. He desires that we would experience the intensity of His Love, His Fellowship and His power. In order to do so, we must come to a place of acknowledgement. First to acknowledge who Christ is and what He has done for us. Secondly, we need to acknowledge that we need Him and without Christ we are lost. The third factor is acknowledging that all dominion is in His hands. The scriptures call Him the Author and the Finisher of our faith. Without him, our life would fail.

Keeping all of this in mind, it is not unthinkable to believe you can have a life that is free. Free to live! Free to move! Free to have your complete being wrapped up in the Master's hands, he who has skillfully supplied all of your needs before you were even born.

The plan of Salvation is simple. It is simple because we only have to choose to serve God. We have to make the decision to either live our life for Christ or not to. Whatever path we take it is ours to choose. The word of God lets us know that no matter what way we live, God is still right there. Even in the midst of that, the hard part is living a life that is designed for God's anointed woman. Many will struggle and battle with denying their flesh. Many struggle with making God Lord over their lives. We struggle with dedication and commitment. Yet, it is not unconceivable to walk and fulfill His purpose for your life without the struggle. Can you imagine that?! We can be all that He desired and more than we thought possible. But, the first step is to choose and embrace God's excellence. Once we decide to come to Him, we MUST allow God to take control of the wheel and stir us in the right direction, which leads to rehabilitation. Yes, Rehabilitation! Why? It is purely because we are all a mess when we first come to Christ. In fact, this is why we come to Him realizing what a muddled web we have sown. God is the only one able to fix it. As a result of the paths traveled, many encountered and experienced situations that God really did not intend if we were obedient. Obedience is better than sacrifice! How we find ourselves making the sacrifice rather than obeying. It is not until after we are kicked around, stomped on and knocked over that we realize this was not the right way. Experience is an excellent teacher. In Luke 22, Jesus began a dialogue with Peter telling him that the devil desires to "sift him as wheat." When sifting, it is a separating or straining process. The devil desires to separate us from God's love to ultimately destroy. Jesus Christ recognizing this goes further to say to Peter in verse 32, "But I prayed for you that your faith faileth not: and when thou are converted, strengthened by the brethren." Peter adamantly declares that he is ready to go to prison or even die for Jesus. At that point Jesus says to Peter that he will adamantly and most assuredly deny that he even knows Christ. Further in the text, Peter does deny Christ three times and immediately on the third time, the cock crows just as Jesus said it would. Jesus looked at Peter and Peter remembered what the Lord spoke to him. Verse 62 lets us know that Peter wept bitterly. It was in that experience that turned Peter around. Not every experience is designed to break you, but rather some are designed to make you. Peter goes on to become a powerful apostle.

When we come to Christ, it is like leaving one hurtful, harmful relationship to enter into a different one, yet bringing the baggage from the old into the new. Psychologists might argue that this is not a good idea. However, this is exactly what God wants. That is why He bids for any to come just as she is. The more jumbled the life the greater the miracle. It is in this down, trodden life - that is no "useful good"- God reshapes and transforms us into witnesses and living examples of His grace and power. The image in the mirror is no longer empty and full of despair but rather full of joy and peace that is desired among others. God makes us functional and fit for His purpose. This is what it means to be rehabilitated. Then we become available for His service.

Salvation is freely given to everyone that believes (Mark 16:16). Salvation is a gift of life that comes only through Jesus Christ (John 14:6). It is the key to your peace, joy and hope. What is Salvation? It is the saving knowledge of Jesus Christ, the point of introduction. Salvation is accepting Christ instead of rejecting him in your life. It is learning and developing a relationship with the Savior. At this point, the veil that was once over your eyes is lifted and we can begin to receive newness of life. Upon the lifting of the veil we are enlightened or made aware of what has been missing in our lives. That void we once felt can now be filled. Salvation makes us available to the will and purpose of God.

With all that crowds our minds, hearts and souls, little room is left to receive the characteristics of God. The characteristics that shape us into the individuals God has predestined us to be. That single mother that worries about being able to raise her child alone and make ends meet or the woman who has been hurt and abused in relationships one after another. It is those very issues that confront us daily and hinders us from reaching our potential. Distractions and other circumstances are weights that pull and slow us down. But one of the awesome splendors of salvation is in all these things we are victorious (Romans 8:37). We can triumph over the devil and life situations. Problems will still come our way, but in the midst Christ speaks peace to our hearts, minds and spirits. Then we are able to continue to do what God requires of us. Paul wrote, "We are troubled on every side, yet not distressed" (II Corithians 4:8).

In addition, we have divine intervention. There is someone to step in just when we need it. Not just anybody, but the Author and Creator of all that does exist or will ever exist. Jesus is our Advocate or the lawyer who pleads and intercedes on our behalves (1 John 2:1). With all these obedience must follow. We must be receptive to the call of God and follow His way. With this plan of salvation, we receive newness of life. Immediately, we become joint heirs with Christ (Romans 8:17). The old character and ways are all replaced with God's character and His will (II Corithians 5:17). That does not mean that you will never make another mistake; but, we have a covering through the shed blood of Christ who promises to forgive us if we ask.

Submitting to what we cannot see and holding on to a word that is not yet tangible is really difficult. Sometimes, it seems down right impossible. But, He will not ask us to do anything we are unable to endure and handle. God will always make it possible and give you whatever you need that you might make it and hold on. We just need to believe it for ourselves. When we lack the faith, we will lack the patience to wait. Prayerfully, the words of this book will find you where you are and provoke you to believe and stand fast to his promises for He will always come through. Let us first pray before we proceed.

> *Father, I intercede on behalf of my saved, sanctified and single sisters. Bless them in deed and give them the desires of their heart. Help them to be strong in the midst of the hardship and to hold fast to your promises and your precious word. Help them to find strength through their worship, service and commitment to you. Give us direction and lead us in the path that you have designed that your will be accomplished. I pray for your continued grace and mercy and that your blood may cover us and keep us from evil. Restore the lost, renew the mind, revive the spirit and exchange joy for sorrow. Illuminate our minds and give us spiritual insight that we may be able to identify the attack of the enemy against our souls. Open up our ears and our hearts that we might readily receive your word and your direction. You are our Creator and our heavenly Father. You are our Redeemer and our Life Line. You are Jehovah and our Wonderful Counselor. All peace, love and joy come from knowing you. Thank you for your blessings and your wondrous, saving, redeeming power. You are both now and forever more, worthy of our praise and adoration.*

> *In Jesus Name Alone,*

> *Amen*

Chapter 1

LET IT GO!

My heart cries and pain floods my soul.
Yet, when I am come into the presence of the Lord,
Victory overtakes my woe.

Proverbs 17:9 (CEV)
You will keep your friends
if you forgive them,
but you will lose your friends
if you keep talking about
what they did wrong.

*L*adies before you do anything you have got to let go of all the past relationships as well as the current ones that are a hindrance. Let go of your fears of being alone, shut off your male detection radar and men alerts, call back the search hounds and tune out your biological clocks so you can enjoy your singleness. It is time to empty out your cup. Right now, your cup of the will is full of past disappointments, relationships not ordained of God, your own agenda, your own desires, fear and doubt. That does not mean you are not saved. It does not mean that you don't love God. It certainly does not mean that it's a hopeless situation. Girlfriend, you are still human. The human . . . the woman in you longs to be held and loved. The woman God created you to be is longing to be that helpmeet and to be appreciated. She wants to be accepted for who she is and wants desperately to remove the mask just so she can be liberated and free. She does not want to worry about what people or he will think of her. When I say he, I do not mean Jesus.

Often times, we try to camouflage what we are really feeling inside with hopes that things will change. However, we need to remember that all the issues that fill our cup become distractions and obstacles to the saved, sanctified woman. They divert our attention from God's intended purpose for our lives. Yet, even knowing this it is easy for someone to say, "Just leave him alone because you can do better." Meanwhile, your feelings and fears hold you there making you feel stuck or trapped. It is easy for the next person to say, "It happened, get over it and move on." However, you know your pain has gripped you so until it feels like strangulation and is a constant reminder of what you endured. It is easy to tell you to wait and trust God; yet, you still feel the pressures of the world around you piling on top and weighing you down. At some point or another, we all go through one way or another. For some, it seems to come all at once or one thing after another. So, none of us are alone and we can all tell our different stories that testify of our struggles and others.

Now, some may think to themselves, "I don't need and I don't want anybody." Have you ever heard that before or were you the one saying it? But, if the truth were told, you are really just afraid of being hurt or that you will never have anyone. So, we build smokescreens as ways to hide our true feelings to protect our hearts. These smokescreens or masks hide the true you, the fearful you, the intimidated you and the fragile you. The smokescreens cover what is broken. But as long as what is broken is hidden, we risk missing the opportunity to be fixed which ultimately results in a changed and renewed life. So, the questions remain. How do I get over it? How do I walk away? How do I learn to wait and trust God for my appointed time?

FIRST STEP: ACKNOWLEDGE

Our first step on this journey is to acknowledge the true depths of our hearts, feelings and intents. When we first come to know Jesus Christ as our Savior, we first admit that we are a sinner and that we need him. The Bible tells us in 1 John 1:8-9 that if we say we have no sin then we really deceive ourselves and the truth is not in us. However, "if we confess our sins, he is faithful and just to forgive us...." We all had to start there. So, before we go any further, we have to somewhat confront ourselves and spread all our feelings, whatever they are, out on the table of our minds. Even when Jesus talks about the prodigal son in Luke 15:11-32, He mentions that the son "came to himself." He thought that my father has so much; yet, I lie here wasting away with pigs. He thought I am going to go back to my father's house. Why? Because he realized what he needed, his father had. Just as the lost son, looked at his current state and realized that there is a way of escape, so must we. Denial works against repentance. It hinders your growth. Denial leads to self-destruction. Therefore, be true to yourself and examine your heart. "Man looks at the outward appearance but God examines the heart" (1 Samuel 16:7 nkjv). You can convince yourself that everything is fine but you will never reach your maximum potential without confession. Take some time to think about what you really feel about yourself and your past relationships as well as your current situations. Take time to think about what your heart really feels and where you are right now. Be honest with yourself and evaluate your relationship with Christ. If you are tired and frustrated, tell Him. Then, ask him to uphold. This must be done to confess or admit to God what you are really dealing with emotionally, mentally and spiritually.

I had to admit that I became angry with God for allowing me to be hurt and disappointed, only to realize that I put my trust in man rather than God who never lets us down. Then, I had to admit to myself that it was a result of my disobedience to God's Word. We reap whatever we sow. If we sow of the flesh, then of the flesh we will reap, bearing in mind that in our flesh dwells no good thing. I had to admit I was in that state of mind because I did not align my own agenda up with the will of God. After that, I had to repent. We kid ourselves to think that we only need to repent once during our Christian walk. But I beg to differ with you. As long as, we are wrapped in carnal fleshly garments, we will find that we struggle, fall short, get side tracked, lose focus and do not always make the right choices. In doing so, we find ourselves getting hurt which does damage to our spirit since sin brings about a separation if not dealt with. This is where repentance comes in and it requires us assessing our lives using God's word in order to align up with His Word.

This type of self-confrontation/examination allows us to admit and to deal with those broken areas such as forgiveness. Forgiveness is not easy, especially when it still hurts. Yet, Jesus tells us that we are to forgive. Even if the same person continually hurts you over and over, forgiveness is still necessary. Matthew 6:14 tell us that forgiveness on our part is necessary if we want God to forgive us of our wrong doings. In addition, 2 Corinthians 2:7 says that unless we forgive, we should be swallowed up by much sorrow. Have you ever or currently found yourself depressed, sad and unable to find peace or joy? Examine yourself and make sure you are not angry or holding a grudge towards someone who may have done you wrong. Grudges, bitterness and an unforgiving heart, will cause us to miss God's blessing in our lives. These also weigh us down. That is why scripture admonishes us to lay aside every weight that easily knocks us off course (Hebrews 12:1). A runner is not clothed with heavy equipment. Imagine Marion Jones, US Olympian Track Gold Medalist, running and jumping over hurdles in football gear. Get that image in your mind because that is what we as Christians do when we worry, carry grudges, feed disappointment and walk in disobedience. Furthermore, David writes in Psalms 66:13 that if we regard iniquity in our hearts, God will not hear our prayers. The method of forgiveness deals with a three-step process. Confront, Admit and Move Past.

1. Confront: What happened, who was involved, why it happened. What was your role and what was your mistake.

2. Admit: Admit how you feel about it and what you could have done differently to that individual and yourself. Resolve the unresolved. Then your healing can begin. Make it right between you and God. In some cases, you may need to talk some people who offended you. You also need to ask for forgiveness for what you did to someone even if it was in retaliation to what was done to you.

3. Move Past: Learn from it and put it behind you. Stop grieving it. It is a dead situation. Anything that is dead should be buried.

We cannot afford to lose what God has for us by living in hurt and living in the past. These keep us bound and prevent us from flowing freely in God's will and purpose for our lives. What is keeping you down or holding you back? They become strongholds. The Greek word is ocurwma (okh-oo'-ro-mah)[1], which means to fortify, a castle or fortress. It also translates to anything on which one relies. Sometimes bitterness and anger are doorways to even more disasters such as sickness. The word of God tells us in Proverbs 15:13, "A merry heart maketh a cheerful countenance; but by sorrow of the heart the spirit is broken." Proverbs later reads in 17:22 that "a merry heart doeth good like a medicine, but a broken spirit drieth the bones." What have you allowed to become your stronghold? Ladies, think about this! Even after everything is done and you have been hurt, the person that hurts you moves on with no problem. Meanwhile, you are still harboring and nurturing your anger. If you do not let it go, it will overtake you and eventually destroy what God wants to birth through you. Hurt and anger are like a pressure sore. A pressure sore is a wound to the skin or underlying tissues that is caused by pressure. With reduced blood supply, this eventually causes cell death, breakdown of the skin, and develops an open sore, which can become infected without the proper treatment and care. In the spiritual, the pressure exerted on our spirit is applied by holding on to those pains and disappointments. It creates open wounds to our spirit man, which weakens our spiritual state. Like a pressure sore, if it is not dealt with it infects your spiritual state of being. Such strongholds need to be treated and pulled down if you are going to grow strong in the Lord.

In 2 Corinthians 10:4, Paul advises us that we have weaponry that is mighty enough to pull down our strongholds. Let's look at ways we are sustained and are changed through Christ the Father:

- Righteousness:

  Romans 8:9-10; 1 Timothy 6:11

  The word tells us that we have Christ and the Spirit gives us life through righteousness. It then tells us to flee from our sins to follow after righteousness. Follow after righteousness means knowing God's laws and being obedient to the Holy Spirit, which will lead and guide us through life's obstacle course. Guard your heart and your mind. Be holy before God as he is holy.

- Faith:

1 John 5:4-5

God lets us know that we as believers are they that overcome and our faith seals this belief so we can stand steadfast. Faith gives us hope and hope helps us make it through another day because we have some positive energy that motivates us to keep going on to see what is in stored for them that know Christ. What would this life be like if we did not have hope? What would there be if we did not have anything to look forward to? Your faith tells you to stand when your flesh wants to give in and when your eyes cannot see your blessing coming. Your faith tells you to hang on a little longer because God is always on time. Your faith tells you do not waver because God will answer your cry. Your faith tells you to wait on him because the latter will be greater than the rest. By faith you stand and by faith you should live.

- Truth:

John 8:31-32

The word lets us know that Jesus says the truth would set you free. The more you know about Him, the more you trust Him. The more you commune with Him, the more you desire to be with Him. Knowing the truth of His sacrifice and His passion brought you to salvation. Truth also deals with being open, honest and sincere with God. Although David was far from perfect, he was still a man after God's heart. That is because of his sincerity and openness.

- Walking in the Spirit:

Galatians 5:16-17

Be lead by the spirit of Christ. We walk in the Spirit by being in tuned with the Holy Ghost and knowing the voice of God. Keep your eyes on Christ and not on people and circumstances. People and various circumstances create blinders. Next, you'll find yourself lost and confused while trying to figure out what is going on and how it happened. Somewhere along this journey, people and things made you lose your focus finding yourself sinking.

- Fasting:

Isaiah 58:6-8

Fast to be restored and uplifted. Fast with a purpose in mind. Fast to be changed and purged. It draws us closer to God. During fasting, it is important to find the time to really seek God's face for his will.

- Prayer:

  1 Corinthians 7:5

  Prayer is your communication with God and the bridge between you and Him. We cannot make it from day to day without prayer.

- Word of God:

  Psalms 119:105

  God's Word keeps and sustains us. It is our map and life's manual. Take the whole Word of God and not just parts of it. Learn and meditate on it. Ask God to illuminate His Word to you and give you understanding of what He is saying to the church through it.

NEXT STEP: PRAYER

Prayer is an essential part of recovery. As we discussed previously, confession is needed for your breakthrough. Let's talk about a very interesting woman. She is known as the woman at the well in John 4. She remains nameless; however, her breakthrough was the doorway, which leads other Samaritans to Jesus Christ. Jesus had a special appointment set up to meet her, unknowing to her. He told his disciples that he had to go through Samaria. As he sat at the well waiting for her, this Samaritan woman began her day towards the well as she might have every day. She had no idea that was the day that would change her entire life. I imagined that she was as many of us from time to time. She was in one relationship after another, not really finding what she needed and not realizing what she needed was not in any man of this world. There were probably many days when it was hard to even get up and face another day because she had to carry the same weights and hurts. Can you see yourself like her? The mask she wore would hide the tears in her heart and the agony of her mind. It would disguise all the emptiness and the disappointment that tormented her daily. We all allow situations, disappointment and mistakes to distress us. However, this Samaritan never knew that day was her appointed time to be freed and changed. We each have a time of sorrow and a time of joy. But we must learn to let go of the sorrow and embrace the joy, peace and strength of God. What is interesting about this woman is how she received her freedom. As the woman at the well talked to Jesus and spent time in His presence, the more she came to know who He was and the freer she became. Initially, her guard was up and she was not completely honest with Him. But the more she allows Jesus to minister to her needs, the more she drew closer to Him. It is amazing to see how Jesus goes right to the heart of the matter and she embraces her deliverance so much so until she ran through the town telling all she could about the Wonder she met. The people knew her, which means something spectacular had to happen to her that brought about such a change in her until it provoked them to want to see who she'd encountered. Her appearance must have changed as the word says in 2 Corinthians 5:17 that when we come to know Jesus, we become a new creature. Plus, true deliverance brings about such a freedom that cannot be imitated with a mask used to cover what is going on in our hearts. When we look at a tree without its leaves and flowers, it really does not look like much. It is not until it buds and blossoms, we see its true beauty. So it endures the harshness of the winter only to be liberated and flourish in the spring. Yes in deed, we all are a mess and go through the storms of our lives. In the midst, God's power is working in our lives to transform us into a work of art to be considered joint heirs with Christ.

The Bible lets us know that her encounter was about the sixth hour of the day. For many of us that sixth hour has come and Jesus sits at the well waiting to embrace you and to deliver you. Ladies, we need the same experience as the woman at the well from time to time. This will help us to deal with our issues and concerns. He wants so much for you to release all your frustrations and anxieties to him and learn to trust in Him only. The more you talk to him, the more you will feel your burdens begin to roll away. Being trained as a social worker and counselor, we find that counseling is essential to help an individual work through their crisis. The counselor wants to find out what that individual or patient is feeling. This is brought out through a series of dialogue, which is needed to diagnosis the problem. Well, take that same mindset with prayer especially since one of Jesus' characteristics is He is a Wonderful Counselor. HE IS THE BEST in the business! You do not have to hide what you really feel and you do not have to put up any smokescreens. What is really great is that there are no misdiagnoses or no misconstrued views. He understands and is there to pull you through.

We need to allow God to take away the stony, harden heart. The word tells us in Ezekial 36:26, "A new heart also will I give you, and a new spirit will I put within you: and I will take away the stony heart out of your flesh, and I will give you a heart of flesh. A perfect analogy is seen in 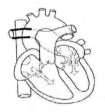 understanding Coronary Artery Disease. This is when arteries become clogged which also refers to narrowing. As I began to research this disease, I found that this narrowing might cause the artery to become as hard as a rock. It is brought on by cholesterol and gradual buildup of plaques in blood vessel but also by injuries to the inner lining of the coronary arteries caused by high blood pressure or possibly infections.[2] Like any muscle, your heart needs a steady supply of oxygen-rich and nutrient-full blood to function properly. That blood is supplied to the heart through the coronary arteries. With any narrowing, a sufficient flow of blood is prohibited and it hardens the arteries. This will eventually lead to a total blockage thus causing a heart attack. Prevention and treatment comes by surgery and medications. It is equally as important for a change in one's lifestyle, such as a change in diet and adding exercise into your daily routine.[3]

In the spirit, amazingly so, the same occurs. Overtime, circumstances, disappointments, hurts and rejection will harden our heart. With either a harden or stony heart, we are unable to be the vessels that function the way God desires to see his daughters flow. It causes us to have a spiritual heart attack. When this happens, God needs to perform surgery on us, thus giving us a new heart. That is why God speaks in Ezekial to say He will remove the harden heart and give us a heart of flesh. Also, David testifies in Psalms 119: 11 that hiding the word of God in our heart will help us not to sin against God. In addition, we must change our lifestyle and our diet. Then, add exercise to your daily routine. Don't feed you hurt. Feast on God's word and His promises. Get your daily dose of exercise. Walking is good for the heart. So, walk in the spirit. Work and faith go hand and hand. Faith without works is dead, (James 2:17). So work while it is day, John 9:4! Take your mind off what was done, why it was done and ways to get back at whomever for what they did. Divert your attention and focus your affection on Jesus so the healing process can begin.

Establish a praying relationship with someone to touch and agree with you concerning issues that confront you. Read the word and meditate on it. Allow it feed your heart and soul. Through it, receive understanding of God's ways and purpose. Establish time for you and God alone. In these times, allow Him to minister to you and give you direction. It is also in these times that God will restore you and rebuild your inner man. At times, we do not know what to even say when we pray. Allow the Holy Ghost to speak for you. He knows what your heart speaks and cries for. This begins your upward spiral or your progressive development. In these times, it is really important that you begin to embrace Jesus Christ. He is the one that will bring you through the hard places and the struggles. If I can grab hold of his word and get into his presence, then I can find the release that I need to move forward in Him. God spoke to me and said remember that He has to be my focus otherwise, all that I see will continuously discourage me and make me faint of heart. But if I can keep my eyes on the promise, than I will be able to see the blessings of God rather than seeing defeat. It is going to take prayer to pull through. Even when I do not feel like praying, I always utter enough to say, "LORD HELP ME!" If I can't find the words to pray, I can always just say, "LORD HELP ME!" Even a baby, knows how to get her mother's attention if she is still unable to speak. Ladies, get His attention. Touch His hem like the woman with an issue of blood. Though she never said a word, she got what she needed from Him. Though she did not have the strength to call out His name, she still pressed pass the obstacles and pain, even with her infirmity and got her miracle. The blood that poured from her was her infirmity. Likewise, our infirmities are our hurts, disappointments, frustrations, angers and lusts. These create wounds that drain life out of us. Our infirmities can debilitate our progression. Our infirmities can keep us from living a fulfilled life. Our infirmities can stop us from obtaining that miracle we so desire, but only if we allow ourselves to be defeated by the infirmity. Do I get angry and frustrated at times? Yes. Do I have moments when I feel lonely and afraid? Indeed. Do I cry, whine and feel like giving up because it gets to hard? God knows, I most certainly do. Yet, I come to realize that these emotional disruptions are variables. They are not consistent. I had to learn not to lean on the variables and not to allow them to become the thermometer of my being. My being is determined by that which is constant. The only thing that is constant is the promises of God. So, when I feel all alone, I know He will never forsake me. When I feel like I cannot make it, I know He will not put more on me than I can bear. When I am afraid that I will not meet anyone, I know He knows the plans for my life. Keep the promises of God to help you hold out.

FORGETTING THE PAST

Paul says in Philippians 3:13-14, "Brethren, I count not myself to have apprehended: but [this] one thing [I do], forgetting those things which are behind, and reaching forth unto those things which are before, I press toward the mark for the prize of the high calling of God in Christ Jesus." Often times, our freedom is delayed because we continually are looking back. Unconsciously, we can try to undo the past through our children and in the decisions we make. For example, parents tend to try to make their children choose careers that they wanted but for different reasons did not go that way. Another example, some find themselves jumping from church to church, neighborhood to neighborhood or job to job trying to escape the mistakes of the past that continue to haunt them. Then, blame it on being bored, needing a change or wanting to start over. Running or trying to escape the past can lead to harsh decisions. If we continually look behind us then we cannot see what is ahead of us. If we cannot look ahead, we become discouraged and lose hope. For many, hope is what keeps us going. Don't let your hope walk away from you. Just know that it will get better than this and trouble will not last always. Keep on looking up and know that this is not all God has in stored for you.

We find ourselves making bad decisions and stumbling over them. That does not mean that you should not remember what God has delivered you from. In fact, remember these as a testimonial of what God can do! According to John 3:33, *"He that hath received his testimony hath set to his seal that God is true."* However, the past should not become a hindrance to your spiritual growth. Paul says I know I have not arrived but the one thing I am sure of is that I am forgetting the past and reaching, yearning and looking forward to greater and better things that God will do in and through me. After all that is done, then my best reward is still to come (Philippians 3:13-14). Paul had to put the past behind him. His past tortured and tormented many Christians. Once God saved him and changed his life, he had to choose to put it behind him. Otherwise, condemnation and guilt would have hindered the work He would go on to do for God. Thus, it would have prevented him from reaching that ultimate place God intended for him. Do not let the past condemn you but rather it should fuel to serve Him more.

There will come a time and a point when each of us will have to deal with the issues that have confronted us throughout the years. At some point, clean the skeletons out of the closet and begin to make the skeletons experiential testimonies that will encourage somebody else. Believe it or not, somebody needs to hear your testimony. Confront your hurt, confront your anger and confront yourself. Get into your prayer closet and into the presence of God. He will show you yourself. You are wondering why the ministry is not moving? You are wondering why you are not progressing? You cannot figure out why you are not blessed? Go to one on one counseling with the Great Counselor. He knows how to go straight to the root of the problem. You can stay there as long as you need and He does not have an hourly fee for his counsel. You want to know which way to turn? You need to know what move to make next? Ask the one who has orchestrated it all.

Forgetting the past means letting go of yesterday and embracing today. It means saying good-bye to your past mistakes and not being afraid to launch into the future of your tomorrow. We allow the past mistakes from keeping us from advancing into the unknown. It leads to fear, mistrust, doubt and anxiety. All of these lead to chains of entrapment, entanglement and bondage. The word tells us not to allow ourselves to be entangled again once the Lord has set us free (Galatians 5:1). Breaking free means disrupting, interrupting and tearing apart from that which has a hold of your heart. Disrupting your current situation means two things have to happen. One, turn it over to God and pull the good out of it. Think positively, begin to ask yourself some thought provoking questions and sincerely answer them. You may not at first be able to answer them but keep asking yourself until you can. What did I learn? How has this experience changed my perspective? If it is pain from a bad relationship, you can turn that bad experience into one to rejoice about. In every bad situation, you can find a reason to be grateful or to simply say thank you Lord.

How can you get the most from bad situations? That is a million dollar question that only you can answer knowing what you have endured. Though it seems virtually impossible to think positive in the midst of torture and torment, it is not impossible. Why? Because you are still here and you are a survivor. When your days should have been cut short, when you should have lost your mind, when could have been wandering the streets, God made a way of escape. He customized your outcome so you could make it another day. In doing so, in your surviving, you have become stronger, wiser and less tolerant of foolishness. It has made you able to better identify situations that are not right and given you wisdom to stay away from them. It caused you not to be so eager to put your trust in the people you meet. It has sharpen your analytical mind and given you a greater keen awareness. Rather than hating the woman you have become and the obstacles that you went through, love her, embrace her and celebrate her. She made it when there were many women before her who never made it this far. In spite of everything, she is still here. There were many women who gave up on themselves and took their own lives. There were many women who fell into the clutches of the wrong person and never got out. There were many women who were institutionalized and cut off from society. But, you survived! You survived for a reason! You have a purpose and God has a plan. Know that all things are going according to His plan.

Every last one of us have a purpose. God desires that we serve him without any distractions (I Cor. 7:35 kjv). Do you think it is by chance you are here? No, not so! Romans 8:29 says that we were predestinated. That means our purpose and reason for being here has already been established before we were even born. That being the case it is up to us to find out what that purpose is. Ultimately, if we were specifically created for a reason and we don't know what that reason is, then we are not fulfilling our purpose. By not fulfilling your purpose, void will exist as we will feel out of place or out of joint. The purpose was put in you. Your purpose is a part of you. For example, computer programs are created for a specific purpose. It was created to produce certain data or results based upon the assessment of the creator and the needs of the customers. If that computer program is not used for its intended purpose and used for any other reason, the results that are produced are useless. Thus, ultimately the program is not fulfilling its intended purpose. We are God's computer programs. He has placed each of us within an environment in order to produce results. If we are not functioning within our predestinated realm, we become useless. Make it up in your mind to find out your purpose. In doing so, you can function within the arena of purpose. It is only in the arena of purpose can you truly find fulfillment and wholeness. Your purpose was designed by the ultimately programmer and He has will provide everything you need to function the way He intends. We must be fruitful to be satisfied and fulfilled. That is part of our programming.

CHAPTER 2

Focus, Focus!

Still and quiet, I must be.
For then my God speaks to me.
Look not to the left, nor to the right.
Trust in ME and lean not to your might.

Proverbs 23:23 (CEV)
Invest in truth and wisdom,
discipline and good sense,
and don't part with them.

Since we are predestinated, God's word tells us to "Set your mind on things above, not on things on the earth", Colossians 3:2. Keep your mind on God and the service He has called you to do. Paul tells us in 1 Corinthians 7:34 that there is a difference between a single woman and married woman. That difference is single women care for the things of the Lord while married women care for things of this earth. As a single woman, God has a specific work He expects to accomplish through her that He would not do through a married woman. So, the ministry of God has to be her main focus. There are certain tasks and assignments that God wants to fulfill in and through her. This testifies of the phases of life within the foundation of salvation.

Salvation is progressive as we grow from faith to faith. This can best be understood in the biblical assimilation of trees. Throughout scripture, Christians are compared to trees. In Isaiah 61:3, we are called trees of righteousness. David said we should be like trees planted by rivers of living water in Psalms 1:3. Jesus calls himself the vine and Christians the branches in John 15:5. In Romans 11:17, He also states that the gentiles were as wild olive trees that were engrafted into the olive tree. So if we think of our Christian life as that of a tree, we see that trees also grow from year to year and mature over time. Trees produce a layer of wood every year of their lives. An Associate Professor of Ball State University says, "The rings that each tree forms are the diary of its life."[4] Once a tree is cut down, we see the rings of that tree, which represents the age of the tree. Some rings are wider and others thinner, depending on their adaptation to climatic changes. Trees that are not subject to different environmental factors determine the complacency of the ring. This means the rings will lack variability.[5] That's in the natural. Let's look at this in the spiritual. If we do not go through our various trials and tribulations, we will not show growth or maturity. If we never go through anything in our lives, how would be learn how to trust Him. If we never go through anything, how would we know that He is a Sustainer? If we never go through anything, how would we know that God is real? If we never go through anything, how would we know that we need him to make it? If we never go through anything, how would we grow into spiritually mature Christians? Even though a child is taught the stove is hot, the majority of children learned what hot meant when they touched it.

Just as trees produce a layer of wood every year, so must we be fruitful and productive within the ministry that God has entrusted to each of us. Then, we can progress and be more of what he wants of us. In each level of faith, there are assignments within the ministry that must be completed and tests that must be passed. The next level of faith is built upon the previous level. There is something crucial in the former that prepares us for the latter. Psalms 1 compares stability to a tree planted by the rivers of water. Her roots go deep and she grows steadily. The rivers of water give her life and strength. She is right where she needs to be to be fruitful and prosperous. We must also find stability in salvation. Get right where you need to be to grow, to learn and reach those heights God has in stored.

STABILITY

It is important to understand that as we live this life, we must be stable and planted just like trees, not contrary and wavering with every wind of doctrine, Ephesians 4:14. Elevation and growth does not promote a double mind. Be consistent in your faith and fixed in your purpose. There are many individuals who fail to receive what God has for them for that season because they are floaters or drifters. They do not stick around long enough to receive the gift or the blessing at the end of that road. The old time cliché says "here today and gone tomorrow" or "sometimes up and sometimes down." The fact is we all go through; yet, we must still run the race with patience and all diligence. Ruth exemplifies a woman with a true servant's heart. A woman of Moab, daughter-in-law of Naomi, Ruth found herself dedicated to Naomi even after the death of her husband and despite Naomi's advice for her to return to her mother's house. As Naomi chose to go back to her homeland, Ruth determined to follow her. She made the decision to leave her kindred and birthplace to launch into unknown and unfamiliar territory. Yet, Ruth trusted Naomi and loved her enough to make this sacrifice willingly, cleaving to her.

Let's think about this woman. Naomi was Ruth's ministry and she walked in it not even knowing what was going to happen. God, in His infinite wisdom, was preparing her for better. But only as she walked in it, could the ministry birth the blessings and favor she would obtain. Through Ruth, the seed of David was born, which eventually led to the birth of Jesus Christ. Waiting on God means being loyal, faithful, committed and releasing one's own self and will. God wants to birth ministry through each of us, but we must be willing to walk away from familiar territory. This is part of expanding our territory. Launch out and trust him. For He is FAITHFUL and will do just what He said He will do. Through the various ministries that are in His daughters, He will save souls, deliver the captive, heal the sick and change our communities and families. But we must walk the path He has chosen and submit to His ultimate will.

See the big picture and see yourself in that picture. God will use each of our lives to push and fulfill His will and purpose. That is one of the reasons why time and season are important to God. God, in His sovereignty, will finish whatever He starts. Ultimately, Him finishing what He starts in you, impacts His flow. It is like a domino effect and chain reaction. Dominos are lined and set up carefully in an organized fashion. All have to be aligned in order for all to fall correctly in its place. The individual setting up the dominos ensures that the surface is a stable and sure foundation, that nothing is in the way that would cause the dominos to fall prematurely and he strategically places each domino. The same occurs in the spirit. God already knows what He wants to birth through each of us. He already knows what it will take to push us into birthing position. The question is whether or not we are ready and willing to take up the mantle? How many of us really have that Elisha spirit that says give me double? How many of us are willing to wrestle for our blessing like Jacob?

We have to be those disciplined vessels of Christ that will not grieve him. Being holy is a lifestyle. Proverbs 25:28 advises us that a person who does not have rule over his/her own spirit is like a city broken down without walls. The walls represent security. They were used as protection against enemies. Without the wall, there is nothing to sustain them, keep them and separate them from outside forces and attacks. This gives the enemy free course to come and go as it seems fitting. The lack of discipline or self-control will only lead to a life absent of God's peace. It is important to find stability basically to grow, for strength and for direction. Stability requires discipline. Discipline comes from setting standards to live by. As we live by standards, we obtain the goals and heights God has prepared. It is a matter of preparation. There are steps and requirements to reach that place prepared just for God's people. We must learn to do what he says when he says. We must learn to give up those habits and ways that will keep us from getting closer to our Savior. What are those obstacles that keep us from the potential that God has in stored? What can separate us from God? It is the sin in our lives. The more sin is present, the greater the gap between the Father and us. It is our responsibility to fight against LSD, Lust, Sin and Death. The Bible let us know that these are the steps toward death. This path is a progressive state of being. First, the lust or desire is conceived. Then, it leads to the sin to fulfill that desire. Finally, the wages of sin are death. We must allow

God to lead and guide us in the way to go. For the word also tells us that there is a way that seems right but the end result is destruction. This downward spiral is the result of a disobedient and undisciplined lifestyle. However, God has created us with the ability to make a choice and thus control our destiny.

A separation can also occur when we fail to seek God for his direction concerning the various areas of our lives. When it comes to making decisions, we often are taking a gamble because we really do not know what is at the end of the path. We can only weigh our options and make an educated guess. But no way you look at it, it is still a gamble because you really do not know what the end will be until the decision is already made. Then at that point, we either did well or regret the decision we made. In such situations, actually in every aspect of our lives, we really need to learn to always seek God's direction because He is the only one who knows the ending at the beginning. He is the only one who can guide. So you say, but what if I've asked and yet I do not hear. Wait on it. He will show you. You may not want to receive it but he will show you.

AVAILABLE FOR SERVICE

Service is the occupation or condition of a servant. A servant is one who performs duties for another. Webster's dictionary goes further to say a servant is a "person devoted to another or to a cause or creed."[6] While working in the vineyard, two things occur. First, it adds to kingdom building and strengthens the ministry. Adding to the kingdom and strengthening the ministry means we are fulfilling God's commandments about service. God says to us through His Word to edify one another in 1 Thessalonians 5:11. Matthew 28:19 says to go and teach all nations about Jesus. Galatians 5:3 says to serve one another in love. Lastly, Acts 1:8 says after we receive power of the Holy Ghost, that we should also become witnesses. Second, service occupies your own mind. Service allows us to occupy ourselves until He returns. It keeps us from fretting about what we have not yet walked in or possessed. It keeps our minds on Christ and it helps us not to focus on what is happening all around us rather than what we find our hands to do.

The songwriter wrote these words:

> *"Lord I'm available to you. My will I give to you. I'll do what you say do. Use me Lord to show someone the way and enable me to say, my storage is emptied and I am available to you."*[7]

Being available means becoming usable. It is the act of freeing oneself.[8] The chorus in this song signifies that an emptying has to take place in order to become available to serve. To become available to serve, self must first die. He states in Galatian 5:24, "And those who are Christ's have crucified the flesh with its passions and desires." Crucified in the Greek is staurow (stow-ro'-o), which means to put to death, to drive down stakes or to fortify with driven stakes. Interestingly, it also metaphorically represents "to crucify the flesh, destroy its power utterly (the nature of the figure implying that the destruction is attended with intense pain)."[9]

Crucifying oneself is never easy. It hurts and there is a price to pay. It will cost us our will and our agenda…our feelings and opinions. However, Paul says it best when he reminds us in Galatians 2:20:

25

> *"I am crucified with Christ: nevertheless I live; yet not
> I, but Christ liveth in me: and the life which I now live in the
> flesh I live by the faith of the Son of God, who loved me, and
> gave himself for me."*

What a radical stance! This suggests we begin to reject our normal way of thinking. It signifies the ability to totally trust God for his will and to give all up to him for his control according to His excellence and sovereignty. It proposes that we lose ourselves in Christ. I mean just get swallowed up in him, recognizing that life truly does not begin until we come to Christ and simply die in him. Ladies, you know how we get when we meet a new man and he is everything you think you have been looking for. We totally forget about our friends and everything else because it becomes all about the new man in our lives. Take that same tenacity, dedication and commitment into a relationship with the Lord. Just imagine the changes that will take place in your life as a result of doing this. New heights, expanded territory, richer blessings, healing, restoration, greater faith and greater fulfillment are awaiting those who dare to take that leap.

How does self die? How do I lose myself and relinquish full control into God's hand? It is a daily routine. Self must die daily as 1 Corinthians 15:31 says, "I protest by your rejoicing, which I have in Christ Jesus our Lord, I die daily."

1. RID ONESELF OF *NEGATIVITY!*

This is a faith walk as the just lives by faith (Romans 1:17). Negativity eats away from your faith. It causes a slow deterioration like rust does to metal over time. Negativity breeds doubt, fear and disbelief. As a result of our disbelief and doubt, we tend to try to be God and move within ourselves. Ridding oneself of negativity and feeding your mind with positive reinforcements promotes spiritual growth and liberty. Reject negativity by the word of God. When negative feedback is given, reject it with the living word of God that refutes what the enemy is trying to hinder. Do not be tools to spread or receive negativity that will destroy your faith for without faith it is impossible to please God (Hebrews 11:6). The Bible tells us in Philippians 4:8 to think on things that are true, honest, just, pure, lovely, of good report. We have to continually guard our hearts and our minds. Ephesians 4:29 says, "Let no corrupt communication proceed out of your mouth, but that which is good to the use of edifying, that is may minister grace unto the hearers." Do not be an advocate of negativity.

2. BE CONSISTENT!

📖 *Be consistent in one's prayers. Be consistent in one's devotion. Be consistent in one's study. Be consistent in one's service.* James 1:6 lets us know that we should ask what we will, but wavering not. One that wavers is like the sea being tossed around by the wind. Battle through the hard and lonely times. Jacob wrestled with an angel all night long for his blessing. His body was full of pain and agony. But he had a determination to get what he needed and knew who would be able to give him that blessing. No matter how it much hurts keep on going and be true to your fellowship with Christ. No matter what happens do not allow your relationship with Christ to be severed. Great is the reward of her who endures the test and trials. But, if she gives up, she will never know what she could have been through Christ.

Remember the adversary is seeking to steal all that God has for you. Yet, we have already been given the victory, we just need to be faithful to the walk by pressing on just as a runner sees the finish line and the trophy at the end of the race. However, the trophy is not received until the runner finishes the course that is set before her. So must we continue the race! Hebrews 12:1 says, "Wherefore seeing we also are compassed about with so great a cloud of witnesses, let us lay aside every weight, and the sin, which doth so easily beset [us], and let us run with patience the race that is set before us." Meaning others have traveled these roads and made it, so can we if we hang in there. At this point in the venture, we are simply fulfilling prophesy, or walking in prophesy. Somebody is asking, "What is she talking about?" Even if you never were called out in service and received a prophetic word, you are still walking in prophecy. HOW? The prophecy was already given through His word through God's promises. Since God cannot lie and His word is never returned without accomplishing or completing what it was sent to do, all of us are simply fulfilling it with every passing day. His word is full of promises and words of hope that still apply to you today. It was not just for the original church, but just as His blood still saves and the Holy Ghost is a confronter, God's promises remain today. He is the same yesterday, today and forever. So your children's children will reap the benefits of salvation. It is the best health plan and employer benefit plan in the nation. Some of those promises say weeping may endure for a night but joy comes in the morning, they that wait on the Lord shall find renewed strength and he will not put on you that you are able to bear. Those kind of prophetic promises that will never change and will carry through the hardships of life.

PERSONAL RESPONSIBILITY

We must accept personal responsibility for ourselves. In today's society, everyone is pointing the finger at everybody else rather than looking at the faults in our own lives. If everyone would focus on bettering themselves rather than their neighbor, this world we be a far better place. But this is not reality. However, the saints can do their part. Often times when we find ourselves being confronted, the outcome depends on our responses. That's why the word tells us blessed are the peacemakers in Matthew 5:9, for only peacemakers can be even considered a true child of God. In addition, understand that a kind word turns away wrath, Proverbs 15:1. When I began my studies in the Master's program at Eastern University, often times we worked in groups on various projects and presentations. We had a saying, "Own your own stuff." Do what you are suppose to do and do not blame someone else whenever you fall short of it.

Whenever we made the decision to follow Christ, we made a commitment to Him. Think of yourself and a friend or boyfriend. You expect that he or she would stand by their words and fulfill any commitments that they make. Likewise, in a marriage, vows are spoken, commitments established and promises made. In order for that marriage to last, both individuals must do their part. Even through the bad times, it is necessary to be faithful and hang in there. If one individual decides not to continue as he/she committed, it causes a strain on the relationship. In addition, it tears down communication and grieves the other. Spiritually, we are married to Christ. The vows we spoke we must fulfill. As a result of our union with Christ, many blessings and gifts were birthed for the ministry. Paul admonishes us to walk worthy of that vocation (Ephesians 4:1). As we walk worthy of our calling, we are as living testaments of God's love, compassion and grace. A consecrated life comes about through discipline and much work. We are living not just to live again but to share the goodness of Jesus Christ with others. Our walk becomes an example for those who we come in contact with us everyday as well as those who will come behind us. If we cannot be committed to our marriage with Christ, then we should question if we are truly ready to be married in the natural.

Think about the time we put in our relationship with Christ, we will discover that many of us are not fully applying an appropriate amount of time into it in order to live the fulfilled life that is promised to us in the scriptures. This may help you in evaluating the time you put into your relationship with Christ. I attended a singles fellowship at my church on February 19, 2005 and the speaker raised some interesting factors about tithing our time[10]. We rarely talk about tithing our time and we primarily refer to our assets. However, we also should tithe our time. So, there are 24 hours in a day and 7 days a week, which totals 168 hours per week. This means we have a responsibility to tithe and dedicate ten percent of that time to God. This means we owe God at least 17 hours per week. It helps to think of it differently every now and then.

God says in His Word that we should not grieve the Holy Ghost (Ephesians 4:30). Still, we do so when we continually fall short of our commitment to Him. We owe Him our life and our worship.

Remember the vow you made to God during your prayer time. Strive to be the blessed and sanctified vessels that God is preparing his daughters to be. Then, we can teach our daughters what God can do in them. Thinking of the ten virgins in Matthews 25, five were wise and five were foolish. The foolish did not have the additional supply of oil. They only possessed what was in their lamps. The wise filled their lamps but also prepared an additional supply as they waited for the bridegroom. When they heard the bridegroom was coming, the foolish virgins ran out of oil and went to buy more oil. However, the bridegroom came while they were gone. When they returned they missed their opportunity to follow the bridegroom who would not receive them. Do not be as the foolish virgins. Do not miss God because you are not are in position or right standing. Get all you can from His Word and stay in constant fellowship with Him. Learn from your elders, teachers and leaders that you may be prepared when your time comes.

You also have a responsibility to yourself. You must maintain a healthy balanced life. If you do not take care of yourself, you will not be as effective in this walk. Get the most of your relationship with God.

1) NURTURE YOUR RELATIONSHIP WITH GOD.

> Fast. Pray. Create special devotional time. Start the day out right so that you can be spiritual prepared for what you will face throughout the course of the day. Continuously talk to Him throughout the day. I noticed that when I do not start the day with devotion, my day is just burdensome. I feel more tired, more consumed by

daily issues and less involved. The whole day just seems to go to the dumps. Pray to make it through the day.

2) TAKE CARE OF YOURSELF.

Eat right. Exercise. Pamper yourself. Find "me time." Get the right amount of rest. Even Jesus found time to rest. Relax and enjoy so that life does not pass you by. Life is too short not to take in moments for yourself and your family, especially if you have children.

3) REMAIN ACTIVE IN CHURCH AND FELLOWSHIP.

When you are going through, it seems natural to just want to hibernate and hide. Sometimes, you wish you could just simply cease to exist. But remember that the devil wants to knock you out for good. If you fall by the wayside, you will give him the opportunity to do just that. But do not give him the victory. No matter what it takes, press your way through and get out and about. Cancel the pity party and tear up the invitations. Whatever you do, do not hang around sad, pitiful people. It will only make you feel worse.

4) REAFFIRM YOURSELF AND WALK IN FAITH.

David had to encourage himself when his followers wanted to stone him after the enemy invaded their camp (1 Samuel 30). Set up some faith reminders of God's promises to reaffirm your faith. When your faith wavers, doubt creeps in. When doubt creeps in, fear comes over. Once fear is there, panic attacks. Then, panic invites frustration and disappointment. At that point, the pity party is long on its way. That is when we make bad decisions and the wrong choices. So, the faith reminders are messages from God's word, which counterattacks the attempts of the devil to make you fall into defeat. Mines are set up in my Microsoft Outlook calendar and flash at certain times of the day. Whatever it takes to get you to hold on, do it.

5) *AVOID MAKING DECISIONS BASED ON WHAT YOU SEE.*

Do not make permanent or lasting decisions based on a temporary bad situation. But in all things, seek God's direction. I was so angry and hurt until I was about to pack up everything and move four states away. I dressed it up real good and called it "starting over." I was not taking into consideration, God's plan for my life and that he has strategically placed me where I am right now for a purpose. Moving in yourself while God is moving is bound to cause a wreck, like two locomotives on the same track.

Consider this! The enemy has to try to stop you. Otherwise, "five of you will chase hundred and [that] hundred of you will chase ten thousand" (Leviticus 26:8). Imagine what affect we would have on the body of Christ and against our enemy if we did not give up! This is a body ministry even with God using our individuality to edify the body and compel others to come. So, what the devil will do is attempt to trap us one at a time, exhausting his efforts to take us out individually. This scripture text leads me to think that by hindering one, he can hinder the redemption of a hundred. Don't be that one.

Each one of us is a construction worker. Each of us is building our own house. We only get one chance to complete it. Even though some of us may have cut corners here and there, you still have the opportunity to correct those mistakes and continue construction according to the blue prints provided in the beginning. This time and space for correction is called God's grace. However, if we continue to cut corners and not follow the blueprint provided, we will find ourselves building houses like the three little pigs. Two pigs built houses from sticks and straw because they wanted to finish quickly so they can play. Only one built a house were he could find rest and security. The first two pigs thought they had it all together and probably thought the third pig was wasting his life away. But there is a way that seems right, but the end leads to only destruction (Proverbs 14:12). The house that you are building represents the life that you choose to live. You can live your life seeking fast results, without following the blueprint of life – the Word of God for man cannot live by bread alone, but by every word that comes from God (Deuteronomy 8:3) -- and in the end you will end up in the midst of disappointment, shame, hurt and destruction…just as the first two pigs who ended up with nothing, literally running for there lives. Or, you can follow the plan of God for your life, abide in Him and allow Him to direct your path just as the third pig. How you choose to live is up to you and your end results will be based on what you sowed.

CHAPTER 3

WARFARE!

We got to fight to stay in this race.
Get into position and keep up at God's pace
Just to see His lovely face.
So we do not ask or do we plea;
But we command that devil to flee.
For too long you've had your play;
Now move and get out the way.

Psalms 144:1 (CEV)
I praise you, LORD!
You are my mighty rock, and you teach me
how to fight my battles.

Spiritual warfare is real. The devil tempts the saints of God just as he did Jesus in the wilderness. He tempts us in the same categories that he did with Jesus. Satan attempts to entice or to draw Christians by the lust of the eyes. He presents it in a way that appeals to us by the way we are or the way we once were. That is why it is important to know yourself, what you can handle and what your interests and habits are or once were. It is equally important to be able to recognize when you are under spiritual attack and recognize the tactics of the devil. As we are able to identify the adversary, it becomes easier to resist and rebuke him. Jesus immediately recognized when the devil was moving or in the midst. He always dealt with the spirit that was working in the spiritual realm rather than who was before him in the natural. That is why it is important for the true believers to walk in the spirit. Walking in the spirit ensures that we will be able to intercede in the spirit and bind those things that would come to hinder us from progressing in the will of God. Part of being spiritually minded means being spiritually equipped and prepared. Saints of God cannot fight a spiritual battle with their natural sight, training and instinct. We cannot come to a spiritual battleground without our spiritual tools and weaponry. That is like bringing brass knuckles to a gunfight. It is useless! Furthermore, we cannot fight in a spiritual battle without being connected to the General.

Ephesians 6:10-18 provides us with a daily routine to fight the devil and to grow spiritually. Verse 10 tells us to be strong, not in ourselves, but in the Lord and in the power of His might. First, we have to recognize that we need him in order to make it. In ourselves we cannot do anything but we can do all things through Christ (Philippians 4:13). Verse 11 tells us to put on the whole armor of God in order to stop the devil in his tracks and verse 12 reminds us that we are in spiritual battle. When someone mistreats us, our flesh immediately wants to respond. But if we remember that we are not wrestling against flesh and blood but spiritual wickedness, we can immediately begin to bind the devil and recognize when he is attacking. Verses 13-17 provide us with the list of the armory and how we are to equip ourselves for warfare. First, know the truth. The truth is we are joint heirs with Christ and seated in heavenly places with him. The truths are we are raised with Christ and have been given authority over every wicked spirit that would try to rise up over you. The truth is we were made to reign over the devil through the redemptive blood of Jesus Christ. We are royalty and God will not withhold "NO GOOD THING" from us who live this life right

(Psalms 84:11). When it comes to my adversary, he has to submit when we command him in Jesus' name. The victory is already ours and was won when Christ raised himself from the dead. Now, we are just walking in that and fulfilling His ultimate plan.

Then, it says to take the breastplate of righteousness. Guard your heart and be holy walking up right. We have to live this life that we preach. Your heart determines who you are. My pastor, Pastor Patricia A. Phillips of Nothing But the Word Deliverance Church, always tells the congregation that what is in your heart is destined to be revealed either in your conversation or in your deeds. Whatever is in you is going to come out. So we have to guard our hearts and pump it with God's precious word.

Third, have your feet shod with the preparation of the gospel of peace. Always be prepared to spread the word of God. Look for opportunities to build God's kingdom. If we are busy working for God, we will have less idle time on our hands. As we spread the gospel of Jesus Christ, we will see lives changed, our community will change and the world will begin to change. Service to God allow us to maintain our focus and not to concentrate on the circumstances around us.

Fourth, take the shield of faith. Without it, it's impossible to even please God (Hebrews 11:6). So, if you do not have faith, it really does not matter what you do because God is not impressed. The moments recorded in scripture that really moved or impressed Jesus were tremendous acts of faith. We must believe in this Christ we live for and have hope in something better than this current life. If not, we walk this road in vain. Faith is anticipation. Faith is expectation.

Now, faith is the substance of things hoped and evidence of things not seen (Hebrews 11:1). Faith tells me that although I do not have a dime in my pocket, I will still be able to open up the business God showed me. Faith tells me that even though I do not understand what God is doing in my life, I know that the latter will be greater than past. Faith provokes me to keep going on despite what my eyes see because I hear in the spirit what God is saying to me. This kind of faith refutes the adversary and renders him helpless because you will not even receive what he has to say.

Next, take the helmet of salvation. Your mind must line up with your salvation and your faith. The word tells us to put away imagination and every high thing that exalts itself above God. Retain the word of God. Lastly, pray always and intercede for one another, persevere and remain in the battle. He will not only equip you but also make you able to utilize those weapons. Prayer - James 5:16: The effectual fervent prayer of a righteous man avails much. To paraphrase: The sanctified and holy one that prays causes situations and ordeals to change. His prayers changes lives, open doors and reverse decisions. This person will make more happen. These kinds of prayers stop Satan in his tracks. These prayers save the drug addict and the alcoholic, never to be addicted to anything other than the LOVE of CHRIST. These same prayers can tear down strongholds and turn an entire nation around. That is why we are instructed to pray and seek God's face in II Chronicles 7:14. And remember, always give Him the thanks. I will let you know a secret. Sometimes, your blessings are entangled or trapped in your praise. Release your worship and adoration unto God and your blessings will begin to unfold. When you just do not know what to do, sometimes the answer is in your worship.

KEEP ME, LORD!

The spirit is so willing, but Lord the FLESH IS WEAK! But in our weakness, HE IS STRONG! Greater is He who is inside of us then they that are in and of this world (1 John 4:4). It is time for us to admit that we struggle with our flesh. We even struggle to do the will of God just as Jesus did in the Garden of Gethsemane. So, what makes us any different? We talked about crucifying the flesh with its affections and lusts. We saw how Paul tells us to die daily. Yet, time and time again, we find ourselves right back in messes, jams and compromising positions. How many times have you cried and prayed for forgiveness, prayed and cried, went to the altar, then cried and prayed some more. It all seems for naught because you continue to stumble. Sisters, you are not alone. There are a whole lot of sisters screaming, "HELP ME LORD!" We must remember that these are trying times and your faith will be tested and tried. Remember 1 Corinthians 6:17-20. I remember the first time, I read this portion of scripture. It truly convicted me. However, when I read The Message translation, my eyes were amazingly opened and I remember thinking, "WOW, what a word!"

17Since we want to become spiritually one with the Master, we must not pursue the kind of sex that avoids commitment and intimacy, leaving us more lonely than ever-- the kind of sex that can never "become one." 18There is a sense in which sexual sins are different from all others. In sexual sin we violate the sacredness of our own bodies, these bodies that were made for God-given and God-modeled love, for "becoming one" with another. 19Or didn't you realize that your body is a sacred place, the place of the Holy Spirit? Don't you see that you can't live however you please, squandering what God paid such a high price for? The physical part of you is not some piece of property belonging to the spiritual part of you.

First, since our flesh is weak, we cannot do it by ourselves. When we made the decision to follow Christ, immediately we became a target for the enemy. That is why we need an anchor, we need a deliverer and we need to be kept. So keep on studying the Word of God, praying and fasting. But while continuing to do so for your spiritual food, exercise some wisdom and make some practical changes in your day-to-day lifestyle.

1   Start by examining your inner circle. We have an inner circle, middle circle that consist of associates and outer circle. The outer circle is those who we come in contact with one way or another but may not necessary know. The inner circle includes family and close friends. These are people with whom we bond. While we cannot choose our family, we can choose our friends and whom we connect with. Your livelihood depends on it. We need individuals in our lives that are taking the same vows as ourselves. We need people who can be supportive of the ministry and the calling within us. We need people who will stand in the gap and intercede, even when a word has not been spoken. Sisters, find people who will be able to become a midwife to you and you to them. We can recognize qualified individuals by their lifestyles and their conversations. If they live and speak contrary to the word of God, cut them off. It may be difficult but it is necessary to be able to maintain your walk. *"A little leaven leavens the whole lump* (Gal. 5:9)." *Likewise, the little foxes ruins the vineyards, our vineyards that are in bloom* (Song of Solomon 2:15).

Pray that God set the right people in your life and He will do it. A close friend and sister in Christ told me she prayed that God would show her who her true friends are. Surely as she prayed that, God began to show her. While he moved certain people out of her inner circle and he began to plant others that she could consider her close friends. Keep in mind that some people where brought into your life just for a specific time and season. Those you start out with may not be those you end with. With any separation, hurt comes whether is by death, betrayal or moves. But know that God knows what is best for your success in this life and is not out to get you. The sooner we recognize when it is time to let go, the better off we will be. Otherwise, holding on causes us more pain and ultimately impact our relationship with Christ. Do not put your relationships and friendships ahead of your purpose. Some may criticize you, say you are conceited and all that comes with that type of criticism. However, remember that you have to do whatever you have to in order to get to the next level. Additionally, two can only walk together if they are going in the same direction. Starting with someone who is going another way is bound to make you more miserable than being alone.

2   Next, realize you are carrying precious, precious cargo - spiritual gifts, the anointing and the ministry of God. You cannot go any and everywhere. Be selective of where you go. Know what is happening there, who will be there and the purpose of the gathering. We even have to be selective about the various church functions outside of your own church. I can recall this same friend telling me about a service she attended while out of town. She saw a sign advertising a church conference with a world renowned minister. She decided to go that evening. However, it

was nothing like she anticipated. Folks were chanting and literally clinging to the walls; the preacher they advertised was no where to be found. Needless to say, she ran out of there as fast as she could. Be mindful that there is such a thing called transferring spirits. Most importantly, be bold in the Holy Ghost. Do not be afraid to change your mind, to say I do not want to go or not tonight. Sometimes, you simply have to say "NO." God spoke to me and told me one day, "Say no and then say why!" I encourage you to do the same. He continued to minister to my heart by telling me not to be afraid to say what heart wants to say in love. My heart is simply doing what the word of God said it would do which is hiding the word that I might not sin. It is when I hear that word coming up – and you know you hear it – that I need to command my actions to fall in line with that word. That is our authority and right to do so! In your proclamation, you may even help a friend.

A compromised witnessed produces a compromised faith in others. They look at your life and think that it is ok to live two ways when in fact it is not. In addition, ladies, lets stop settling for any man just so we do not have to be alone. It is worse not to be aligned with God's Word and disobedient because you are in a relationship with the wrong man then to be alone and in right standing with God. That man will be there but your fellowship with Christ will become tarnished and tainted. If you are wondering if he is the one for you, first you need to ask yourself these questions: Is he saved? Does he serve your God? Can I tell he is saved by his lifestyle and does his walk produce the fruit of God? If you can answer yes to these questions, then ask yourself what God is saying? Can you date? Yes, of course but be lead of God when you do. Now, for some of you, this might be outside of your norm. This might not be what you usually do. However, these times are calling that we make drastic changes and change the way we think and see our relationship with the Lord as vital to survival.

3   Lastly, we need to guard our hearts, spirits and minds. God spoke to my heart to challenge you to make a physical note of all your actions/habits the past week; holy and unholy, positive and negative, good and bad…more specifically as it relates to your fellowship with Christ. After, you make that note and highlight the unholy, the negative and the bad. Now do not faint when you see what a mess you are because we are all as filthy rags before a clean, holy and righteous God. If we weren't, we would not have needed saving. Focusing on one at time, keep it before God through pray and fasting, determined to change them. Learn what the word says about it. Pursue holiness no matter what it will take. Do this every week for the next three months and you will begin to see your life changing right before your eyes as it is done in sincerity. Why? Because you are making a conscious effort to change. You are "intentionally turning around." Whenever something is done intentionally, it is done deliberately and on purpose. Keep in mind your purpose and change will come. God will make the change.

A RENEWED MIND

More than half of our battles begin in our minds. The way we think and the thoughts that Satan plants into our minds are the doorways to passing or failing our test and trials. That's why the New Testament authors continually admonished the need to guard our minds. Romans 12:2 says, "And be not conformed to this world: but be ye transformed by the renewing of your mind, that ye may prove what is that good, and acceptable, and perfect, will of God. Ephesians 4:23 goes further to say, "And be renewed in the spirit of your mind." 1 Peter 1:13 speaks to us saying, "Wherefore gird up the loins of your mind, be sober, and hope to the end for the grace that is to be brought unto you at the revelation of Jesus Christ...." We have to continually pray that God will cover our minds. For many, the mind is the devil's playground. He feeds it with thoughts of defeat and negativity. Immediately, we need to reject the thoughts that the adversary plants with the word of God and by exercising the God given authority that every believer was issued when Jesus Christ died on the cross. Everyday we need to pray that God will keep our minds, after all, HE IS A MIND SUSTAINER! Let's be honest. If he wasn't, some of us would have lost it a long time ago. Thank God for his sustaining power!

Kenneth Hagin suggests in his "Believer's Authority" that if we are not going to walk in the authority that we have then Christ died for nothing.[11] Besides that, we will not know what we have until we use it. Pastor Allyn Waller, of Enon Baptist Tabernacle, ministered to a multitude of about 200 or more people on Tuesday afternoon in Downtown Philadelphia, Pennsylvania. His topic of discussion was about love taken from 1 Corinthians 13. Pastor's Waller's message was strong and compelling. But one thing that stuck out most in my mind was when he began to expound on verses 9-12. Paul writes:

> "For we know in part and we prophesy in part. But when that which is perfect has come, then that which is in part will be done away. When I was a child, I spake as a child, I thought as a child; but when I became a man, I put away childish things. For now we see in a mirror dimly, but then

44

*face to face; Now I know in part, but then I shall be know just
as I also am known."*

Pastor Waller lets us know that prophecy and all use of the gifts
are for now, here on this earth because we truly do not know the full
picture. So, the gifts are for the perfecting of the saints through Christ
Jesus. In the operation of the gifts, we can encourage one another and
lead others to try him for themselves. We will not need these gifts
when we all get to heaven. You will not need someone to give you a
word; after all, the KING himself will be right there.[12] Likewise, the
authority that Jesus transferred to us is for right now. It is time for us
to recognize this and begin to walk in that authority.

What is this authority that both these men talk about? It is the
power of Jesus Christ that He transferred to us before He ascended and
sat on the right hand side of God the Father. It is walking in Christ
and knowing who you are. It is identifying what keys we hold in our
hands. It is like receiving keys and directions to specific location and
being told how to get there, what you see is yours. Unknowing to you,
these keys are to the mansion of your dreams. However, if you never
walk into the home, you will never claim it as your own. Just because
you cannot see the authority does not mean that you do not have it. It
just means you have not used it. This means we have authority over our
minds and our flesh. Paul writes:

*Romans 7:23-25 says, "But I see
another law in my members, warring against the law of my
mind, and bringing me into captivity to the law of sin, which*

is in my members. (V. 24) O wretched man [woman] that I am! who shall deliver me from the body of this death? (V. 25) I thank God through Jesus Christ our Lord. So then with the mind I myself serve the law of God; but with the flesh the law of sin."

What this says to me is that I recognize that there is another force working against my mind and my will and it is within myself! I am really a mess! It will lead me right into the bondage and captivity of sin. BUT, Thank God Almighty through the precious blood of Jesus Christ who gave me the authority and power over this flesh and who sustains me through His every word. So, I choose to live free from sin and bring this flesh captive to the will God. That is what kind of authority we have through Jesus Christ! I had to learn to walk in this authority. It does not make sense to receive all the benefits of the kingdom and all its rewards; yet, continue not to use them. I can think of another analogy using keys. Suppose a parent gives her child keys to go into the house when he or she returns from school. While the mother is on her way home after work, there is a major storm and immediately she remembers her child has the key to get in the house out of the storm. However, when she arrives home, the mother finds her child sitting on the stoop outside in the midst of the horrific storm She can't help but wonder why? I say to you why not use the authority you have? Why stay caught in a mess that God has already delivered you from, yet the adversary wants to keep you bound in your mind through condemnation? Why give up when you do not have to?

How is it that we are called joint heirs with Christ, seated in heavenly places, the head and not the tail and power over all the works of the devil but still walk in defeat? God is calling us higher to take our rightful position. Many of us are still suffering from our slave mentality. Meanwhile, we have been moved from the slaves' chambers or our imprisonment just like Jehoiachin, King of Judah who was taken prisoner due to disobedience. Yet, he was later seated at the royal table. 1 Kings 25:29 says, "So Jehoiachin put aside his prison clothes and for the rest of his life ate regularly at the king's table. Day by day the king gave Jehoiachin a regular allowance as long as he lived." Let's take it a step further and say you received power and authority the minute you sat down at the table. Check this out...all you have to do is just say the word. God says to speak it!

Stay There: Peace in the Storm

Paul talks about the grace of God. He found that God's grace is sufficient in the midst of the infirmity. He found that his current state, hardships and trials are not worthy to be compared to the Glory that will be revealed to them that love and trust God (Romans 8:18). In times past, we as believers were taught that we should not question God about what is happening in our lives. We were taught that if we ask why or what is happening, that we do not trust God and that we sin in doing so. But on the contrary, it is unrealistic to think that you will never holler out...WHAT IS GOING ON? Even Jesus on the cross, suffering, carrying the sin of the world, cried out in Matthew, "Why has thou forsaken me?" During Job's suffering, he said in chapter 3 that he is the one that long for death but it just will not come to him.

I remember going through at one particular time in my life. I did not want to pray because I knew all I would do is complain, cry and moan. I wanted the burden lifted and I wanted to move out of this place, but I did not want to pray selfishly. The devil will plant anything in your mind to keep you from getting your breakthrough. When I finally found myself in my prayer closet, all I could do is cry and ask why and when. He did not speak a word and did not show me a vision. God did not send someone to encourage me. In fact, there were times when I found myself getting up with no change in my attitude or the way that I felt. The more I prayed, nothing changed and I did not get a response. So, I felt it was not necessary to even pray. Though I felt the urge to pray, I would not because accepting where you do not want to be is not easy, whether it is a result of disobedience or place of transition. Yet, I found a place of release when I began to search the scriptures and meditate on His promises. It was then I realized that His response never changed in the midst in the trial…"My grace is sufficient." My faith was just not receptive to the word that was spoken to give me life.

Paul asked God to remove the thorn from his side three times and each time God said no. The last time, God told him that His grace was sufficient. That encouraged Paul. Paul had a breakthrough. Though the situation did not change, Paul changed as a result of it. That is what needs to happen to us. The situation does not always change because we are the ones that need the change. God is just trying to make us better. Since that is the case, we need to be able to take the heat. We need to be able to stand the pain and we must persevere. PRESS! Philippians 3:14 says, "I press toward the mark for the prize of the high calling of God in Christ Jesus." The word press is dioko (dee-o'-koo) in the Greek. It means to make, to run, to pursue (in a hostile manner) or run after swiftly.[13] What does it means to press?

> ***Persevere*** through the pain: Be stedfast in your purpose and continue in your efforts despite hardship, difficulties, shortcomings and tribulation.

Resist the devil's mind tactics of defeat: Resist the devil and he will flee or run away in terror. Do not allow him to rob you by planting defeat and negativity into your spirit, James 4:7.

Encourage yourself: Begin to meditate on the word of God. Remember His promises and what He has already done, 1 Samuel 30:7.

Stand still: Be disciplined and unmovable, faithful and consistent.

Seek God's face: Pray, fast, read the word of God and be renewed in his presence.

David wrote in Psalms 27:13, "I had fainted, but I believed to see the goodness of the Lord in the land of the living" (kjv). He goes further to say in verse 14, "Wait on the Lord: be of good courage, and he shall strengthen thine heart..." David writes in the past tense in verse 13 by saying he had fainted. This leads to believe he already gave up and already turned away. Let's think about it. David was anointed to be king over Israel long before he actually walked in those shoes. He went through some rough places and I am quite sure that he went through some dry places. Saul was trying to kill David, so he was on the run. It was not just anybody that David had no dealings with. Saul was his king, his father-in-law and his best friend's father. In some instance, perhaps Saul was like a father to David. Yet, Saul was so jealous of his anointing that he wanted David dead. I imagined he was just about to walk right out the door. But just as he opened the door, he began to think of all the promises God made to him, which caused his faith to testify and stand up in him. David comes back to say, "But I believed to see the goodness of the Lord in the land of living." If we lose faith and hope, we will not have anything to look to or expect. Imagine going through life without ever expecting anything positive to occur. Sometimes, in the midst of a situation, we can speak to ourselves that this is just "a means to an end." I need to go through this to get what God has for me. David did not actually possess the promise in the natural but he believed to see God fulfill his promises right here on earth. Just begin to think to yourself, right where I am. God is going to fulfill his purpose in me right where I am, in the land of the living. God is going to do just what he said he would do. I am going to walk in every blessing, gift and anointing that my God has prepared for me here on earth.

Another thought taken from Matthew 14 where Jesus walks on water. Picture the text in your mind. The ship was in the midst of the sea and a monstrous storm. The waters were violent and the winds atrocious. Along with the rains, I imagined it be as frightful as being in the midst of a tornado. While trying to manage and survive this storm, the disciples look out and see a figure walking towards them on the water. As if the storm was enough, they became even more afraid. But just as they thought it to be a spirit of some sought, a voice tells them not to be afraid. The voice sounds familiar but it cannot be the Master. It is humanly impossible to walk on water. So, Peter dares to take a chance. He says Lord if it is you, tell me to come to you. Jesus simply replies, "Come' (v 29). Peter steps out on the water and begins to walk on it, right in the midst of the storm. Before, he even realized it; he was already out the boat and in the midst of the raging storm, walking on water towards the Master. But what happens, he starts focusing on all that is around him, becomes distracted, begins to panic and fear takes over; thus, he begins to sink. Can you see in the spirit the exact same thing happens to us in our Christian walk? Can you hear God saying to us come on, I gave you your instruction, now get out the boat and come on? In our zeal and excitement with some hesitation, we step out on faith walking toward the mark. Then, the devil throws all kinds of obstacles at us to distract us. He realizes that he cannot pull you down unless you are distracted. It is not until we become distracted that we can see what is happening around us which challenges our faith. But I admonish you to recognize that the miracle already began. You are already walking on water! You are already out there in the midst of it all; yet, God has sustained you to get to this very point in time. Put the devil in his place and KEEP GOING!!

Unwavering faith is a gift and we are not all fluent in our faith. It is natural to feel like giving up. It is natural to feel like you cannot make it. It is natural to become so burdened until you cannot see a way out. But if we remember this one thing, these feelings are all in the natural and in our flesh, which always yearns to do the opposite of the God. But our faith is supernatural and sees beyond what our natural eye sees. Faith enlightens the spiritual eye and helps us to see what God is perfecting. Even when you feel like your faith has packed its bags and moved next door, remember God is moving in your life two important ways. First, by our faith...look at the centurion who asked Jesus to heal his servant by simply speaking it. Jesus was amazed by his faith and honored his request (Matt 8:9-10). Secondly, there are times when God moves strictly according to his plans fulfilling His promise. Just take a look at Isaiah 55:11. The Message translation writes, "So will the words that come out of my month not come back empty-handed. They'll do the work I sent them to do, they'll complete the assignment I gave them." Look at Sarah who laughed when she heard the angel of Lord say she would conceive a son. Even though she did not believe it, the Bible tells us that at her appointed time to conceive, she surely conceived. The overall plan of God was created and included that she would conceive this seed of promise. I am so glad that God's plan supercedes my faith. I know I would not be where I am if it was always up to my faith. So that in itself should help to increase our faith. God will do just what he says! Let me say this...if you have been waiting for God to do what He said He was going to do, you ought to begin to break out in a crazy praise because you know He is committed to His word...EVERY WORD! It does not matter what it looks like or what it feels like, change is coming...it is on its way. That's the truth and you do not need a prophecy to know that.

In the midst of your struggles and frustrations, remember what Christ has done for you. Remember what He endured that you might have a right to walk this way. Remember how Christ suffered, bled, died and gave Himself as a sacrifice that you could receive the un-repayable gift of life He provided through His blood sacrifice, all so you can enjoy the fruits and rewards of having entered a relationship with Him. Hebrews 12 reminds of this very fact. The Message translations says:

> [1]Do you see what this means--all these pioneers who blazed the way, all these veterans cheering us on? It means we'd better get on with it. Strip down, start running--and never quit! No extra spiritual fat, no parasitic sins. [2]Keep your eyes on Jesus, who both began and finished this race we're in. Study how he did it. Because he never lost sight of where he was headed--that exhilarating finish in and with God--he could put up with anything along the way: cross, shame, whatever.

And now he's there, in the place of honor, right alongside God.
³When you find yourselves flagging in your faith, go over that
story again, item by item, that long litany of hostility he plowed
through. That will shoot adrenaline into your souls!

After reading that, how can you just walk away and quit? How can we just lose heart and faint before we even obtain the blessing that Jesus already paid the price for? That is like being given a brand-new Mercedes Benz, but you chose to continue driving the old beat up Jalopy because you do not want to go through the process to get it. Don't get deep and say you would not want it or that is vain or materialistic. Please, I cannot imagine being given a Mercedes, S-Class with all the trimmings, all expense paid but I fail to go through the process to obtain it. Just show me what I need to do and I guarantee it will be done. Of course, the process is not easy. But can't you just see yourself sitting in your Mercedes. Well, it is the same thing in the spirit. The price was paid and then we were admonished through the scriptures what was needed to obtain our rewards. Of course, the best reward is in heaven. But he also promised us much success if we obey his word, despite the hardship that occupancies doing God's will. It worth the struggle and it's worth the fight because there is nothing like enjoying the fruits of your labor. See yourself enjoying it, now before you even get it.

CHAPTER 4

THE LOVER OF MY SOUL!

Philippians 3:7-14 (CEV)

7. But Christ has shown me that what I once thought was valuable is worthless.

8. Nothing is as wonderful as knowing Christ Jesus my Lord. I have given up everything else and count it all as garbage. All I want is Christ

9. and to know that I belong to him. I could not make myself acceptable to God by obeying the Law of Moses. God accepted me simply because of my faith in Christ.

10. All I want is to know Christ and the power that raised him to life. I want to suffer and die as he did, 11so that somehow I also may be raised to life.

12. I have not yet reached my goal, and I am not perfect. But Christ has taken hold of me. So I keep on running and struggling to take hold of the prize.

13. My friends, I don't feel that I have already arrived. But I forget what is behind, and I struggle for what is ahead.

14. I run toward the goal, so that I can win the prize of being called to heaven. This is the prize that God offers because of what Christ Jesus has done.

Song of Solomon 5:9, 16 (CEV)

9. Most beautiful of women, why is the one you love more special than others? Why do you ask us to tell him how you feel?
16. His kisses are sweet. I desire him so much! Young women of Jerusalem, he is my lover and friend.

What greater love is there than that of a man that would give his own life for a friend...for someone that did not even know he existed? Love is a strong word and used so often prematurely. Love is often converted to perversion and used lightly. The world makes you think that true love can only be manifested in sexual acts of passion. Often people confuse love with lust and have not really had the opportunity to really experience true love. But true love bears pain and suffering. True love stays when every one else goes. It is deep and passionate affection towards another person. It is a feeling that stirs up devotion and loyalty. You cannot truly love a person without having the opportunity to know them and spend time in their presence.

Think back on one of the best relationships you had with someone. What made it so great? What was so wonderful about that person? What did you love about them? Well, imagine that Christ is so willing to have that same relationship with each of us. He wants us to know him in such a way we feel like we simply cannot make it without Him. The difference with Christ is that he will never let you down and never walk away from you. The difference is He is so forgiving and will not hold your mistakes against you. If we can know Him, just as he knows us...if we could embrace who he is just as he does us, we would find that Jesus is truly the lover of our soul. What is so great about that is He wants to be. Unlike those times when we tried to make someone want to be with us and love us. Ever been there? Doing all you can, going over and beyond for someone that just simply does not love you back. It is exhausting and heart-breaking. Trying to keep up with him, always making yourself available and continually neglecting yourself to please him. Girl, the more you do, the more you have to do and more inconsiderate of your feelings he becomes. In our relationship with Christ, he is usually the one we reject. Knowing how it makes us feel, we can empathize with the grief we repetitively cause Him. When we would give up on others, He does not.

What is it about this man that He keeps on taking me back after countless times that I have strayed to seek out my own way or a so-called better way? Why does he continue to love me after I constantly break his heart? I simply had to know him better. In knowing him better, I see the Man that he really is and then begin to desire him more.

I WANT TO KNOW YOU

It seems that so much is required of us along this walk. Often we hear people say salvation does not cost you anything. This is true. But to live this life will cost us something. Just as any relationship will cost us something from time to time. Continually, we chose to please our loved ones even when it is not what we really want. At times, it is hard to disregard the feelings of a loved one to please yourself. So what do we do, put our own feelings and desires on the side burner to satisfy someone else. Yet, when it comes to our relationship with Christ, we find ourselves doing the opposite. But if we came to the place in Christ where we really truly know Him, we would find it is hard not to want to please Him the more. However, it is hard to conceive knowing someone that you cannot physically see and touch. It is hard to comprehend having a relationship without a physical person. But to differ, Christ is so real and you will only find out just how real he is if you experience him. Go ahead ask me…what are you talking about experience Him? How do I experience Him? In a relationship with Christ, you will experience His touch, His power, His blessings and His transformation. In a relationship with Him, you will see Him move, heal, deliver and many other miracles. In a relationship with Christ, you will hear His voice, counsel and learn His wisdom. Over all, you will experience the difference that God makes in your life when you accept Him.

Truly, experience is the best teacher. You can look back over your life and testify that there were situations when you were told not to do something but you still thought you should. You were convinced that this was the best thing to do…it was what you needed to do. Nobody could persuade you otherwise. Yet, in the end you found that it was one of those decisions you can only look back at now and regret. But you have to kind of appreciate the experience because it has in some way changed your perspective. So that now, when you speak on the subject, you speak from experience. You speak about what you know to be true after living and surviving it since the greatest witnesses are survivors!

I think about myself and I remember that fearful and intimidated person. I still see her from time to time. I recognize her insecurities, her doubts and her hesitation. I needed to know God not just as a Redeemer but as a God that would be strong for me…a God who would carry me. That is what I can say God is to me. We have to get to the place where we can identify what God is to me. Everyone else's testimony is great and even inspiring. But since I lived in doubt and fear, those impediments gobbled up the word sown and testimonies heard as if it did not apply to me. Then, disbelief and a lack of confidence became my mentors. Ladies, I needed to know a God that was there for me. Thank God for what he did for everyone else, but I needed a personal visitation and experience with God. Not one that I heard about but one that became my reality. Only when you go through and endure can you find that element of the relationship that helps you identify what God can truly do. Now I know because He delivered me from there and some. Likewise, the more you think about your personal experiences and what God has done, you will begin to see Him different and acquire a different enthusiasm and longing for Christ. Your experiences with God will bring a passion that only time can produce. Time spent in his presence, time meditating, time learning his word and time enduring the rough places.

A Sunday school lesson or Sunday morning message cannot give you the Christ encounter you need to know Him in a way that provokes you to devotion. It will encourage you and it will provide you insight. Often we think because we go to services and participate in various religious functions that we are fulfilling our Christian duties. On the contrary, we need more than rituals and fellowship. We need more than once a week feeding. We do not feed our physical bodies once a week and we certainly should not feed our spirits just once a week. Studying God's Word will teach us what we need to survive. Then applying its principles to our daily lives helps us to grow. It is in the growing that we begin to experience the richness of knowing God.

There are four principles to remember in your pursuit to know Christ better.

- ### HE WOOS AND YOU RESPOND.

  Christ draws us. Think back on the times you felt compelled to pray, read your word or fast, even in the middle of the night or outside of your normally scheduled times. Think of the times you felt led to intercede for someone, go to a particular service or listen to a sermon on the radio or television. Your response becomes the meter that measures our depth in Christ. It will determine how far you will go in him. The more you respond, the closer you will get.

- ### GET YOUR FEELINGS OUT THE WAY.

  We cannot judge by the way we feel or allow it to interrupt our movement. Do not allow how you feel to be the matrix for determining your altitude in Christ. There will be times when you just do not feel like praying, worshipping or going to church. This does not mean you are saved or that you are out of place with God. Sometimes, we can go through so bad until it seems like a punishment. Our feelings about our situations are not consistent. Sometimes, we feel like running through troops and all that. But other times, we feel like we are being pounded on and unable to make it to the next day. Yes, our feelings fluctuate and sometimes you will feel like you are simply crazy. "Emotional breakdowns" are temporary and you can not base your faith on them. But, remember that God's Word never changes from day to day. What He said he will do and is able to perform. Despite your hung down head, God is still in control. So, press pass, put your feelings under subjection and learn how to command your body to line up with your spirit. I tried it and let me tell you it really does work! There were times when I just spoke to those oppressing spirits that want to rob us of our joy and peace. In the name of Jesus Christ, they have to get back into their place. But rest assured, these spirits will continue to try to keep you from touching the Father any way they can.

- *SEEK DIRECTION AND GET SUPPORT.*

  Continually seek God for his direction. He will show you what he wants of you and he will lead you accordingly. The scriptures admonishes in Matthew 7:7-8, "Ask, and it shall be given you; seek, and ye shall find; knock, and it shall be opened unto you: 8 For every one that asketh receiveth; and he that seeketh findeth; and to him that knocketh it shall be opened." In all that you do, connect with people that are like minded with you. Such people can pray and encourage you at the same time. Even Jesus gathered disciples to accompany him.

- *ENDURE THE TRIALS AND DARE TO EXPLORE*

  *T*he trials act as building stones or blocks. These become those incidents that help us to identify with just how awesome, great and powerful our God truly is. It is one thing to read that Jesus healed the woman with an issue of blood, opened blind eyes or made the lame to walk…But it is an entirely different story to know that he has healed you from Multiple Sclerosis or dried up your mother's cancer. Your witness changes when you experience His deliverance and redemption first hand. Likewise, it will make you step

out more in Him…trust Him more…desire Him more…
dare to explore. It awakens a faith like no other that can
only be birthed through trials and tribulations.

LISTEN AND YOU WILL HEAR

How many times were you speaking to someone and you got
the feeling that they just were not listening? How nerve racking is that?!
What is the usual response? "Are you even listening to me" or "You
aren't even listening." How about the times when you have to keep
repeating yourself because the person that you are speaking to is simply
not getting what you are saying? That, too, can be rather frustrating.
Well, I imagined that's what we constantly put our God through. But
thank God, He is more patient than we. Many, many times, we say God
is not speaking to us or we are waiting for Him to direct us. Yet in fact,
He already spoke and in some cases, more than once. It is time to fine
tune our ears to hear what the spirit of God is saying. Not only to us
individually, but also corporately. We need to be connected to Christ,
the source. In addition, we also need to be connected to the church we
serve and fellowship in, to its leader and its vision.

Mark 4 talks about 4 different kinds of hearers. As we look at
them, examine yourself and determine which you are.

- *FRIVOLOUS HEARERS:*

  v. 4, 15 – Scriptures describe this person as the one
  who hears the word however Satan immediately takes it
  away by force. It never gets planted or rooted. So this
  individual will not grow and become stagnate. This is

because that individual is not receiving the nutrients vital to their spiritual health, which promotes growth. Just as the natural body needs food to survive, so does our spiritual body/man. The frivolous hearers need to learn how to clear their atmosphere so that they can receive the word. Before you read the word, pray and command your atmosphere to be cleared. Even in church, command that atmosphere to be cleared and ask God to open up your hearing so that you are not dull in your hearing.

- ***FRAIL HEARERS:***

  v. 5, 16 - The frail hearer is described as one who hears the word, yet it does not go deep. It is only good for the moment that it is received. So when trials and problems come, because it has not penetrated the heart of man, the frail hearer does not endure and is not steadfast. This is the individual who continuously falls along the way, finds it nearly impossible to overcome temptations, defeated in trials and always giving up. They are not consistent and lack discipline required for this walk. The frail hearers need to make up in their mind whether or not they are in it and going to go all the way. Determination is missing characteristic of the frail hearers. Do you want to walk this walk or do you want to the things of the world. You cannot have both so which one will it be.

- ***FAINT HEARERS:***

  v. 7, 18 – These hear the word but without focus, they are unfruitful. Faint hearers get caught up in all that is going on around them rather than holding to God's Word.

These are the ones whose faith is depleted by circumstance. Faith comes by hearing the word of God (Romans 10:17). Faint hearers need to get all the word that they can. Get to church, bible study, read it on the train, in the tub… By any means necessary. Get into right fellowship and get rid of the weights and baggage, whoever or whatever they are…especially those that transfer a negative spirit as negativity is infectious and highly contagious.

- ### *Flourish-able Hearers:*

v. 8, 19 – Good hearers are the ones that receive the Word of God. They use it to look at themselves and find direction through it. They hold on to its truth and stand in faith, regardless of what is going on around them. For this reason, they can flourish and yield much fruit.

We must learn to listen to God when he speaks to us and give us direction. In order to do this, we must recognize when God is speaking. He speaks to us to show us his way. He speaks to us to encourage us. He speaks to us so we will no go astray and that we will understand His ultimate purpose for our lives. God wants to reveal to us the mystery of salvation and what he desires for each of us. Understand that there is no revelation, however, he will reveal to each of us differently and at different times. God appropriately divides out a proportion of knowledge to us a little at a time, depending on what we can handle. Therefore, as he decides to reveal, he will speak to us in four of the following ways:

- ### *Through His Word.*

The word is "the revealed will of God…the message from the Lord, delivered with His authority and made effective by his power."[14] In the word of God is described in many ways throughout scripture.

o *Sword of the Spirit – Ephesians 6:17*

o *Quick and Powerful and sharper than two edge sword – Hebrews 4:12*

o *Mirror – 2 Corinthians 3:18*

o *Light and a lamp; Instruction and Guide – Psalms 119:105*

o *Son of God (Jesus) – John 1:1-18*

o *Nourishment – Matthew 4:4*

- *THROUGH VISIONS.*

  In Acts 2:17, Peter quotes Joel when he prophesied that in the last days that through the endowment of the Holy Spirit, men would see visions and dream dreams. He goes further repeat Joel in verse 19 saying that God will show us wonders.

- *THROUGH OTHERS.*

  The gift of prophecy is the divine empowerment to speak or to foretell events as it pertains to the mind of God. God has placed such gifts as prophecy and word of wisdom and knowledge within the body of Christ to encourage, provoke, direct and edify his people according to his divine purpose. What is so wonderful about it is that God will always confirm his word, which is spoken to you.

- **DIRECTLY INTO OUR SPIRIT.**

God will speak directly to our heart and our Spirit. We do not need an arbitrator or that third party person to reach the heart of God on our behalf. Jesus became the propitiation and our atonement. He is all we need. Additionally, God is our God. We talk about this relationship being personal. That being the case, why should our God speak to someone else rather than speak directly to us?

SEEK HIM AND FIND HIM

To seek means to search or to look for. Scripture urges that if we ask, we will receive. If we seek, we will find and if we knock, the door will open. Often times, we speak about seeking the face of God through pray, fasting and by reading the word of God. But we also must learn to seek God in a different way, which may require a paradigm shift for some of us. I say that because, many times we say we believe God will provide yet we stress ourselves trying to figure out ways to make ends meet. We say we believe God will make a way out of no way. Yet, we are in the way trying to create our own plan of action. How many times, do we just say well "God you allowed me to be in this place and I believe you allowed it to be so just so you can show off in my life. So I will seat back and wait." It seems nearly impossible to wait on God. It seems like He simply takes His sweet time to deliver us when we are going through. It seems like the more we sweat and worry, the longer it takes. I use to really stress about making ends meet. One day in pray, I said God I know you are my provider and I cannot pay what I simply do not have. I refused to stress about it. And believe it or not, I just stopped. It was not until I let it go, that I began to see how God was always already meeting every need and paying every bill. Understand what I am testifying. He ALREADY paid every bill each month while I continued to pray and cry what is going on! For the tears and the fear, I could not see what God was already doing for me. The scripture says take no thought about tomorrow. Just believe that God has provided in the past and will continue to do so.

We need to realize that seeking God is believing God. Seeking God is trusting God. Seeking God is waiting on God and seeking God is expecting God to show up and perform. My child asked for a new video game since He received all A's on his report card. He asked because He knew I could do it. I do not believe he would have even asked if He did not think I could do it. Likewise, like most children, he asked when I would give it to him. I said I could not give him a specific date but I will definitely get it. Believe it or not, he did not stress about it even though he asked for it in the beginning of June and did not get it until the end of July. Just as a child believes that their parents will provide and does not stress about what their next meal will be or whether or not they will have clothes to put on or a place to sleep, we must also believe that our Heavenly Father will always make sure we have everything we need. Additionally, if we did not believe that He was able we would never ask in the first place. Why should we even ask in the first place? If we believe that God will answer our prayers as scripture declares, then we only just need to ask. Then, worship Him for hearing our prayers.

To seek also means to pursue or go after. It is not enough to sit back and wait for something to happen or fall into your lap. Sometimes, we have to go get it. God may promise you a job, house or car. But we have to go look for it. Certainly, it will not just drop into your living room. You can desire an education and a degree, but only by attending classes and passing the test will you reach that goal. This is not a "Houdini" faith or "I dream of Jennie" walk. We cannot just bob our heads and all our desires are fulfilled. It takes faith and work. Now, we can argue that God will give us whatever we need and he does not need our help. Too often we get in the way. This is true. However, we still have a responsibility to do whatever He tells us to do. Sometimes, He directs you to go to a specific place or He may tell you to wait because it will come to you. In any case, we have to be sensitized to the leading of His spirit, thus knowing what directives God is giving that we may follow them wholly.

Seeking involves four major components. They are desire, inquire, require and acquire. First, to desire is to want, to long for or to yearn. Whether your desire is to know Him better, to have a better job, to get married, to be debt free or to acquire wisdom, the will or desire begins the process to receive. The will or the drive will generate the request. This leads us to inquire of God or to ask God. We all go to God with some desires both spiritually and naturally. In prayer, we make our requests known, whether for ourselves or for those around us. As we pray to God, he communes back with us making His will known to us. He gives us directions and lets us know what He desires of us and what we must do to reach those goals. After, receiving His directions, the third step is to follow what God spoke into our spirit. We are required to be faithful in following His word. To many times, we fall short of doing what he spoke. Then, we cannot understand why it is taking so long or why we still have not received what God said we can have. We hold up our own blessings by being disobedient. Only when we follow his plan do we acquire. Lastly, when we acquire, we need to rejoice and show God our gratitude.

CHAPTER 5

RISE UP!

Stand up to the challenge and rise to the occasion.
Fear not the course chosen neither despise the affliction.
Chosen, Predestined, Set aside and Justified for His Glory.

James 1:12 (AMP)

Blessed (happy, to be envied) is the man who is patient under
trial and stands up under temptation, for when he has stood
the test and been approved, he will receive [the victor's] crown
of life which God has promised to those who love Him.

You have been appointed for the task. Now the question is…Are you up for the challenge? Esther was given the opportunity and the position by God to make a change for her people. Initially, when the opportunity presented itself, her faith wavered and Esther doubted her purpose. It was her Uncle Mordecai that caused her to examine herself and to realize that God had appointed that hour to use her for His glory. In realizing this, Esther willingly stepped into the realm for which God had already ordained that she would walk gracefully in to fulfill. God will not put more on his daughters than that which they are able to bare. He will not put his daughters in any position to use them without the tools, gifts and wisdom to do so. But most importantly, He is able to work through her even with her downfalls and shortcomings. We must be willing to step into the supernatural territory of God. It is in the supernatural where we see miracles take place, the impossible becomes possible and the unthinkable becomes attainable. We step into the supernatural whenever we step out on faith. Without faith, Moses would not have been able to become the catalyst used to deliver the children of Israel. Without faith, Gideon would not have trusted God to defeat the Midianites with only three hundred men. Certainly without faith, the woman with the issue of blood would not have been miraculously healed.

It is time for the women of God to take a radical stance like never before. It is time to recognize the end-time hour. It is time to declare it is necessary to change and become avenues for that change. God is looking for those who will step up and rise to their call, recognizing that He has so much more in stored for them that accept His call. Obedience is better than sacrifice. When we do not walk in God's will, think of all the sacrifices that we make. Either we will obey or we will find that we sacrifice our peace of mind and forfeit our joy just like Jonah. It seems easier to just be obedient but it is not always easy to actually do when we add our own agenda into the mix. My mom use to tell me, "You'll make out better if you listen." So, that time has come to decide whether to just obey and trust that God is in control or to sacrifice.

Imagine that an intruder comes into your home. Then, he challenges you while he is causing havoc and disrupting your life. You have the means to stop him and you have the authority to remove him. What will you do about it? Now see this same scenario in the spirit because this is exactly what the devil does in our churches, our homes and in our communities. Ladies, I ask again…what are you going to do about it? Think about when you were a child, were you the type to run from a fight when it came to you or did you defend yourself? Were you always the one picked on and did you let them pick on you.

Did your parents ever threaten you to defend yourself and fight back? The Kingdom of God suffers violence and the violent takes back by force, (Matthew 11:12). It is no time to lay back, become passive and unresponsive. Ladies, we can get militant and still be beautiful, holy, sanctified and graceful. Why? It is simply because we do not war after the flesh, (2 Corinthians 10:3). But rather we war in the spirit, in the supernatural where we can be the most effective and do the most damage. Again, our weaponry is not carnal, but mighty through God.

STIR IT UP

The old time saying "Great things come to those who wait" is so true. But even more than that, great things come to those who press for it, work for it and strive for it. The greater the effort the greater the blessing. Often times, we fail ourselves by not making an effort and by not motivating our faith to works. The woman with a severe blood condition, tried all she knew and spent all she had on doctors to help her. When she realized that her help could only be found in one person, Jesus Christ, her faith motivated her to press her way to the master. Picture this scenario in your mind. She had to be tired and weak, yet she pressed. She had to be in pain, yet her faith stirred her to act. So through the crowd, on her knees, she managed to just get close enough to touch the hem of Jesus' garment. Immediately, the bible tells, that Jesus felt virtue leave his body. That was healing virtue that healed her instantly. What a powerful and wonderful example of faith! We need only to look at this woman as ourselves. Yes, I am going through. Yes, I hurt. Yes, I am at the end of the rope. However, if I can hang on just a little longer. If I can press a little further. If I can just touch only the hem of Jesus' garment, just enough to get His attention, just enough to get the power of change to flow through me, I can make it and it will be all right. My situation may not change but His grace is sufficient enough to sustain and cause my faith to grow that I may stand. When we can get to the point that we can touch Jesus with our faith, immediately, we get Jesus' attention. Remember, tremendous acts of faith will move God and cause a reaction.

The disciples said to Jesus how can you asked who touched you when there is a mob of people surrounding you and touching you. But, Jesus told them there was something different about that touch. It moved Him. The true worshippers know how to move Jesus. Why, because they worship Him in spirit and in truth. It is not just praise with the lips with no lifestyle that follows. But it is true devoted worship that rings from the hearts of His daughters. It is that kind of worship that is rendered with a pure heart and clean hands. That's why David wrote "create in me a clean heart" in Psalms 51. This same one with clean hand and a pure heart will receive the blessings and righteousness of God, Psalms 24:4-5. Let us step into the kind of worship that says, "Lord, I will serve you because I love you and because of this love, I am bound to serve you." No matter what the situation, God will bring us through it. But we must continue to press on despite what it feels like or what it looks like. Just know that God it in complete control.

Faith is the substance of things hoped for and the evidence of things not seen (Hebrews 11:1). It is what motivates us to believe and to act. So we must stir up our faith to cause a reaction to take place. A reaction is a response as to a stimulus or influence[15]. It is not responding by instinct but rather it is responding as a result of something that occurs or happens. Faith is the stimulus. Faith will cause you to press on despite obstacles. Faith will make you stand when everyone else around you faints. Faith will push you into heights unknown and cause us to be as Abraham to call those things that are not as though they were (Romans 4:17).

Ladies, it is time to wake up the warrior in you that has been lying dormant for too long. Meanwhile, Satan continues to shift you as wheat. We need to recognize what hour it is, get into position and begin to fight back. We have to become militant in the spirit. I thought about activists and rebels. These are groups of people that are true to a cause. Sometimes, you will find that these groups are so committed to their cause, until they begin to launch attacks. How many times have you heard about violent extremists? Well, though we wrestle not against flesh and blood but against principalities and spiritual wickedness, we need to become extremists in the spiritual realm. It is time to just begin to blow up some stuff, tear down some walls and let the devil know we are here to stay. This day and time is calling for extreme measures and a serious mindset. You cannot beat the devil playing games with him because he is not playing with you. Whenever you are under attack and feel threatened, it is only natural to fight back! Well, we are surely under attack and it is indeed time to fight back. Your very existence is being threatened and your life depends on you fighting back.

How can you fight back when you are hurting and wounded? How can you fight back when you don't know how? How can you fight when all your strength is gone? How can you fight when you've lost the zeal to live? These are legitimate questions. I had to ask myself these very same questions. After being hurt so many times...when you are simply just numb without any passion for living...confused, exhausted...merely existing and going through the motion. Sad to say, many of us got caught up in the "robotic syndrome." We simply ceased to enjoy our salvation and appreciate the life that God has given us. It hurts you say, we all have been hurt but God is a healer. The scriptures let us know that by His stripes we are healed. That means fully, completely and wholly healed, even in our emotions. Researchers are discovering that a broken heart is real. It seems that being emotionally hurt can cause actual damage to the physical heart. These researchers of John Hopkins University are discovering that "sudden emotional stress can also result in severe but reversible heart muscle weakness that mimics a classic heart attack." [16] So, not only can a situation affect your emotional state, but it also affects you physical body. That would explain some of your tiredness, headaches and chest pains. Some situations can literally knock you off your feet and can affect your entire state of being. But, researchers also state that your body heals over time. Ladies, it is time to receive your healing. God is speaking to you and saying to be renewed in your spirit right now! Now you are wondering how do I become renewed in spirit and begin to live again? Ezekiel 16:4-8 (amp) reads:

> *"And as for your birth, on that day you were born your navel cord was not cut, nor were you washed with water to cleanse you, nor rubbed with salt or swaddled with bands at all. No eye pitied you to do any these things for you, to have compassion on you: but you were cast out in the open field, for your person was abhorrent and loathsome on the day that you were born. And when I passed by and saw you rolling about in your blood, I said to you in your blood, Live! Yes, I said to you still in your natal blood, Live! I caused you to multiply as the bud which grows in the field, and you increased and became tall and you came to full maidenhood and beauty:*

your breasts were formed and your hair had grown, yet you were naked and bare. Now I passed by you again and looked upon you: behold, you were maturing and at the time for love, and I spread my skirt over you and covered your nakedness. Yes, I plighted My troth to you and entered into a covenant with you, says the Lord, and you became Mine."

You have a reason to live simply because you entered into a covenant relationship with God and became His. Just when you thought nobody cares, God begins to speak to you and He is speaking to you now saying that He knows and He cares. Daughter, it is so time to live again! I dare you to stop right now and begin to rejoice and praise God for being true to his covenant and His promises. Thank him for loving you even though you rejected him. Thank him that you are still here and for giving you this opportunity to live again. Thank him that through it all you can still stand up and live to fight another day. As you begin to repent for giving up and not trusting God, I dare you to begin to rebuke the adversary and say what God says that you are. You are an over comer, you are victorious, you are joint heirs with Christ and you have been clothed with His righteousness! He will not withhold any good thing from you and God is faithful to complete the work that he started in you.

STAND IN THE GAP

We are living in perilous and wretched times. It will get even worst for we know that the Bible has already warned us of these terrible times that we are living in. As a result, the church is on duty and on call. However, many of us lay asleep and are not even aware of the attacks of our adversary. We continue to argue with one another, tear down each other and bring dissension in the midst of what should be harmonious, well balanced and uplifting. It is sinful how we allow the enemy to cause discord and strife between the children of God. We must remember that salvation is like a water faucet. It does not turn on and off at our leisure. Instead, we walk in it daily and it flows continuously. We should not waver and neither should we be vessel of destruction rather than restoration. It is time for all God's daughters to begin to intercede for her sister, mother, brother, children and father. Since the devil is busy, we need to become even busier, focused and determined to bring down his kingdom. What should I do to promote change?

📖 BE A WITNESS!

There are two types of witnesses. We should be both.

1) LIVING REPLICA: - MATTHEW 5:16

Be holy as the Lord your God is Holy. Several times, the scriptures admonish the saints to be holy and walk upright before God. Without holiness, we cannot see the Lord

(Hebrews 12:14).

2) VOCAL ADVOCATE - MATTHEW 28:19

The Bible tells us to spread the gospel of Jesus Christ. We have been commissioned to win souls for the kingdom. Through our lives and our testimonies, others can find redemption through Jesus' saving grace.

📖 PRAYING!

Always remember to pray for them around you.

1) FOR YOUR ENEMIES:

"But I tell you: Love your enemies[a] and pray for those who persecute you,"

(Matthew 5:44).

2) FOR THEM THAT MISUSE YOU:

"Bless those who curse you, pray for those who mistreat you"

(Luke 6:28).

3) LEADERSHIP:

"And do not forget to do good and to share with others, for with such sacrifices God is pleased. Obey your leaders and submit to their authority. They keep watch over you as men who must give an account. Obey them so that their work will be a joy, not a burden, for that would be of no advantage to you. Pray for us. We are sure that we have a clear conscience and desire to live honorably in every way."

(Hebrews 13:16-18)

4) FOR GOD TO SEND LABORERS TO THE MINISTRY:

"Ask the Lord of the harvest, therefore, to send out workers into his harvest field."

(Matthew 9:38)

5) THAT YOU DO NOT FALL:

"Watch and pray so that you will not fall into temptation. The spirit is willing, but the body is weak."

(Matthew 26:41)

6) ONE ANOTHER AND HEALING:

"Therefore confess your sins to each other and pray for each

other so that you may be healed. The prayer of a righteous
man is powerful and effective ."

(James 5:16)

📖 FASTING!

In Matthew 17:21, Jesus lets us know that some things can
only be handled by prayer and fasting. Some of the areas in
your life will not be changed without fasting. Fasting becomes
your spiritual portal since it is in this we are humbled and
purged. We are dealing with spiritual wickedness and forces
in high places. That being the case we must be spiritually
minded and filled in order to handle them. That untapped
territory will be overtaken through fasting and prayer.

📖 SERVING!

Service helps to occupy your time. The bible tells us in
John 9:4 to "work the works of him who sent us while it is
day." Having the mind of Christ means we must become
servants. All while Christ was on the earth, He served.
As a child, he said he had to be about His Father's business
when His mother asked where He'd been (Luke 2:49).

1) SERVE ONE ANOTHER: GALATIANS 5:13

We can serve one another by being an encouragement.
We are suppose to edify, love and uphold one another.

2) SERVE GOD: JOHN 12:26, ROMANS 14:18

There are many blessings in stored for them that serve
him. However, our service and commitment is driven

by our love for the savior. In fact, everything we do should be motivated by our love for God. Not to receive acknowledgements from man, but because we want to and we have a desire to serve him. This type of servant is a bondslave or servant. This is someone who acts out of their desire to want to please their master. The Greek word is doulos (doo' los)[17].

3) SERVE YOUR PASTOR: *II KINGS 2*

Elisha became devoted to Elijah. Elijah was his mentor. He saw him as a teacher and father. In doing so, Elisha would leave all else to follow Elijah wherever he would go. He knew him and believed in his ministry. As a result of his dedication, the mantle of Elisha's leader fell on him. Others identified the spirit of Elijah on Elisha through the power of God. We must also dedicate ourselves to the ministry and the leaders that God has planted each of us under. By doing so, you will not only reach the heights that God has in stored for you but you can also be a blessing, support, a help to the ministry and to that leader.

CHALLENGED

Here is the scenario. The thief, who is our adversary, comes to steal, kill and destroy (John 10:10). When you know a thief is on the prowl, you will prepare yourself. You do not know when the adversary will attack or how, but you can always be prepared. The object is to recognize him when he does. We can best do this by walking in the Spirit. The Word encourages us to walk in Spirit that the righteousness of the law might be fulfilled in us (Romans 8:1). It also says walk in the spirit not to fulfill the lust of the flesh. The word admonishes us to resist the devil and he will flee.

Recognize that there are five major components of prayer that we need to incorporate into our pray life. These areas create a sure foundation that effectively positions us for warfare. After all is done, listen and allow God to speak to you heart. He definitely will minister to your needs and give you direction.

WORSHIP:

The Bible admonishes that we should enter into his gates with thanksgiving and into his courts with praise. God loves worship so much that he has set up angels that worship him nonstop. We have to create an atmosphere that is as inviting as the atmosphere God is accustom to, which makes him want to inhabit those praises. Make Him feel welcomed!

CLEAR THE ATMOSPHERE:

We need to clear the atmosphere of all demonic forces that are established to hold up your blessings, directions and answers. Imagine a telephone conversation that is full of static or where you can hear other people's conversation. How nerve-racking is that?! That is what the devil attempts in the spirit realm. He devises so much chaos to hinders the answers from reaching their destinations.

INTERCESSION:

It so important that we begin to intercede for one another and hold up one another through our prayers. Every last one of the saints is under attack. Therefore, it behooves us to look out for one another. Additionally, the bible admonishes that we should pray that God would send in laborers...saving the lost (Matthew 9:38). I began something new. I began to pray for others when I began to worry about situations in my own life. Worry defeats faith. So by me praying for someone else, I divert attention from myself and at the same time I am helping someone else who is need of a breakthrough.

REPENTANCE:

We need to continually ask God for His forgiveness. When I was growing up we were taught to say, "God forgive anything I said or done that was not pleasing both known and unknown." Then, I just did it because that was what was taught. Today, I say it because I need the Lord to "create in me a clean heart and renew a right spirit in me" (Psalms 51:10). We need to remember to pray for our secret faults (Psalms 19:12)...Those hidden idiosyncrasies that no one else sees but we know. Remember God sees and knows all. So it does not make much sense to act like everything is in order when we know it is not. God loves sincerity and openness. When we come before him naked, he will provide a covering, which is the blood of Christ. Be covered by His precious blood and not guilt, shame or self-righteousness, which prevents the cleansing from occurring.

REQUESTS:

The bible tells us to let our request be made known unto God and that we have not because we ask not. There are some guidelines, you must have faith. JUST ASK! THEN BELIEVE! YOU WILL RECEIVE! He is diligent to respond to all them that believe in the name of Jesus (1 John 5:13-15). For without faith it **is** impossible to please him: for he that cometh to God must believe that he **is**, and that he **is** a rewarder of them that diligently seek him (Hebrews 11:6).

CHAPTER 6

CELEBRATE!

Now, with this thought in mind, I will rise to celebrate.
Faith believes all things and hopes all things without hesitate.
For I am royalty appointed for this hour and endowed with His power.
So I rejoice for the Lord is my help and my strong tower.

Now Ladies, let's just celebrate. Celebrate being a woman, more importantly a woman of God. Celebrate being a vessel that God has sanctified and raised up for this end time hour. Celebrate the liberty where Christ has made you free. Celebrate your singleness and the fact that you can be content in it. Celebrate that God has not forgotten you; but rather, he redeemed you to be a witness and an encouragement to your fellow sisters who were once like you. Celebrate that you are not like you use to be; but, that you are a work in progress, changing daily for the better as you walk with Christ and submit to His will.

"The best is yet to come" one songwriter writes[18]. You have not even begun to see what God will do in and through you. God wants us to become those vessels that he can work through you and not just in you. Once the pathway is cleared and the house is in orderHe can freely flow the way God desires. Many trials and test will continue to confront you but you must hold on to God's promise. Be encouraged as James 1:2-4 admonishes:

"My brethren, count it all joy when ye fall into divers temptations; Knowing that the trying of your faith worketh patience. But let patience have her perfect work, that ye may be perfect and entire, wanting nothing."

The potter is working on you, the clay. Isaiah 64:8 says, "But now, O Lord, thou art our father; we are the clay, and thou art the potter; and we all are the work of thy hand." Sometimes the potter has to press down on the clay to form it into His likeness. At times, the Potter needs to trim down the clay in one area and increase the clay in another. In all that the Potter does to His sculptures, the clay never moves, complains or resists. Allow Him to work on you and to make you into the woman he desires you to be. Stop fighting the process. Go through so you can grow. He just wants to perfect you.

Victorious Living

What does it mean to be victorious? It is overcoming obstacles, being triumphant in battles...simply, having good success. The key to victorious living is SWEAT. I know what you are probably thinking. What in the world is she talking about? First, understand that we cannot achieve good success without doing something to get it. It will not just happen. There is some work that is required of us. "To whom much is given, much is required" (Luke 12:48). I am reminded of the Master who gave his servants talents in Luke 19:11-26. At the end of the parable, the servant, who did not multiply his talents, lost the one he had. It was given to the one with the most. Work with what God has given you and he will do the increase (1 Corinthians

3:6). Still confused about what SWEAT means. It is quite simple. Submit, Worship, Expect, Align and Trust. This mixture will ensure that you walk victoriously, have good success and become productive. We've continually looked at submission, expectation (otherwise faith and hope) and trust. Now, let's take a deeper look at worship and alignment.

When we talk about alignment, we are really speaking about understanding what God wants from you, knowing what He says in His word and simply doing it. It is imperative to be in the right position with God to effectively grow and produce in God. Last Christmas, my son received a 10 in 1 Game table. This game table was not assembled. So, my father and I decided to work on it while my son was asleep. When we opened the box, we found instructions, which provided step-by-step instructions and pictures as well as a list of tools needed to complete this project. First, we needed to align the legs with the table top, which had pre-established holes to screw in the bolts. There was an additional tabletop, which would be used for Foosball. In order to place this on top of the Air-Hockey table, there were holes on the side of the Air-Hockey table and holes on the side of the Foosball table. The first challenge was putting together the Foosball table. We had to align the walls/sides with the bottom/playing field. To do this we had to put the playing poles through the sides to hold them while sliding the bottom into a grove at the end of the table. If it was not set up properly, it would dip down, making one side of the bottom lower than the other. This meant the ball would gravitate to the lower end of the table. I hope you are seeing the picture spiritually. All this was mentioned to say this; as long as we are not aligned with our Creator, we will gravitate to a lower level, thus missing out on God's ultimate plan for your life and not maximize our potential.

Worship is defined by Webster's dictionary as extreme devotion or intense love or admiration of any kind. In the spiritual realm, worship is a lifestyle. Worship is what we do in every aspect of life. Not only is worship is performed by lifting up our hands telling God how wonderful He is and singing a song, but true worship is living a obedient life before God, acknowledging him for direction and wanting to continually be in His presence. We worship because we love him. When we are in love with someone, they best know how we feel by the deeds that we do and not just by what we say. We worship Christ in our submission and witness. We worship Christ by completely giving of ourselves. I did not completely understand people that used the term, "I am worship." Oh, but now I do. My Christian life is worship to God. It brings him pleasure and He inhabits it. It is true I could not express my love for God in words alone. But perhaps, an obedient, submitted and surrendered life shows Him more than my words could ever. Webster's says that worship is love and admiration. That being the case, just us loving God is worship. The true worshippers are those that live the life. The true worshippers are those that intimately embrace their God. Not for reward or favor; but, because they love him.

He Knows the Plan for Your Life

Life is but a moment and we all have an appointed time on this earth, after death is judgment. But during this life we can always live a dead life, spiritual life. Whatever path you choose is yours to do so. That's why scripture admonishes that He knows the path we take. God is not surprised by our actions and our thoughts. Psalms 139 lets us know that He knows what we are thinking before it even comes out of our mouth. It says no matter what way we live whether it is for God or not, He knows and He is there. Though we have the propensity to grieve and disappointed Him by our choices and lifestyle, God is still not surprised. Being shaped in iniquity as David writes, we have a sinful nature that desires to do its own thing whether pleasing to God or not. The flesh just wants to be satisfied. Because of this, we often do not make the right choices, yet He knows. We are so busy seeking fame, fortune, acknowledgement and riches that we forget about our souls and eternity's destination. However, God knows ahead of time the path that you will take. Because of our distractions and own agenda, we miss God and the opportunity to grow by leaps and bounds. These are missed opportunities to really know God, missed opportunities to walk in true freedom and missed opportunities to live a full and abundant life. Yet, he knows. Keeping this in mind, God has so orchestrated His plan that will cause your missed opportunities to work out in your favor.

Missed opportunities, broken agendas and torn relationships from God create voids in our life and cause spiritual death overtime. God spoke to Ezekial to tell him that he would bring Israel back together as a nation after they were scattered abroad for their disobedience. He told Ezekial that the Children of Israel do not deserve it but He was going to do it because He wanted to get glory out of their life. God wanted people to recognize that He is God by looking at Israel's life example. God, as merciful as He is, wants to do the same thing in each of us. He wants to get the glory out of your life, as messed up as we can be. He wants to fix us so He will be recognized for His greatness. Just imagine someone that is laying out in the gutter, dirty, smelly and utterly in the lowest state possible in life. Along comes Royalty and sees this desolate individual. He takes her in, cleans her up and turns her life around. He basically needs to deprogram her way of thinking that has been imbedded in her for years to make her a new person with a new attitude and outlook on life. That being case, it is inevitable that she stumbles and does not always do things the way He likes but He knows what she will be when He is finished working on her. Despite her mistakes and her imperfection, He continues to genuinely love, nurture and bless her. The more he is there for her, the more she realizes how much she needs him. After all, if she had it all together in the first place, she would not need Him. Even recognizing that she needs Him, she still does not do everything right the first time, even the second or third time. But, He is patient and forgiving, continuously upholding her as long as she stays under His covering. That is the kind of God we serve. He is that Royal gentleman that sees a rose garden that has been neglected and uncared for; yet, He envisions the beauty of its splendor for the entire world to see and behold…Just to stand in awe of its wonder. There is nothing as beautiful and intriguing as a well cared for ROSE GARDEN. LADIES, WE ARE THOSE ROSES. With all our differences and uniqueness, we represent the various natures of those roses.

He knows what is best for you and the plans for your life. When you do not understand everything, He knows. When you fall short and frustrated with circumstances, He still knows. When you feel like giving up and throwing in the towel, I am so glad, He knows. So what you are struggling with right now, He already knows and is going to work on you until you can overcome it. That situation that seems to be working against you, He knows that too. He is right now, pushing and wooing you to your open door and way of escape. Believe it or not, He already knows and has already made provisions that allow space for our mistakes so that his plans for us are not destroyed because He will not allow one word He has spoken to return to him void. HE WILL do whatever it takes to make sure that His word is fulfilled. So if he has to move some stuff around to do it, He will do just that.

One morning on the train ride to work, I began to read the story of Lazarus, Martha and Mary. Although, I read this portion of scripture many times, I found God began to speak to me. Jesus loved Lazarus and when he received the news of his condition, I can imagine that it was of no surprise to him because he knew the end results and what his plan was for this situation. When he received his message, he did not drop everything and go running. He waited for the right time. When Jesus arrived, Lazarus was already dead. Martha ran out to meet Jesus. In her anger, hurt, disappointment and frustration, she confronted Jesus by telling him if you were here Lazarus would have not died. After Jesus' dialogue with Martha, he ends up telling her that He is the resurrection and life. Martha then in her shame sends Mary to Jesus. Often times, we respond to Jesus in prayer out of anger and frustrations, which does not show our trust in His plan and who He truly he is. This is why Jesus had to open Martha eyes so she could realize who she was actually speaking to. When Mary approaches Jesus, she fell at his feet and said what Martha said. Immediately, Jesus was moved with compassion and only said but one thing, "Where have you laid him." As I read that I could feel my spirit welling up because he revealed to me something powerful. Somebody today called on God and they did not get an answer. Let me say this to you. It is not that he did not hear you and that he will not respond. It is that he

89

is waiting for the right moment to show up…when it is dead. Then, He can get all the glory out of the situation. But keep this thought in mind. If he does not come when you first call him, stay humble. Do not allow the devil to embitter your heart because God knows what is best for you. Otherwise, when you enter into a dialogue or prayer, you will not be in the right position. Mary said the same thing Martha said. Yet only Mary moved Christ to compassion. That is because Mary was in a different position. She positioned herself humbly and in a place of worship. She spoke from her faith. Mary spoke from her relationship with Christ and based on the time she had spent with him. She remembered just who He is. Although, Jesus did not come right away, she said I know that you are still able. In the midst of every situation, no matter what it looks like, remember who God is and what He can do. Remember that He has the plans for your life already taken care of so that you may receive your expected outcome. Remembering will position you into a place of worship that will allow you to move God.

God began to show me some distinct features about his plan. It is really a set up. Think about it. He set up Job so that Job would obtain a greater testimony and a closer relationship with God. The purpose of His set up is to take you from your pit to your palace. In doing so, He teaches us to trust Him, it increases our faith and it causes us to look to no one but Him. There are two sides of the paradox…God's intention, which is the set up and Satan's conspiracy. The paradox is that God uses Satan's conspiracy -- to discredit, discourage and destroy you -- to ultimately bless you and bring you closer to Him. The Master has every intention to take us from our pit to the palace. We can look at Joseph, who was a man anointed by God; yet, despised and hated by his brothers. In the midst of his slavery and imprisonment, he continued to obtain favor, he continued to prosper and he continued in his anointing. God will take care of his own, even in the midst of the imprisonment and hardship. The paradox is amazing in that God has so devised his plan that we can only succeed even though we are in the midst of troublesome times. Our adversary is limited and does not have free course in our lives. All he does is within the confinement of what God allows. In addition, God will only allow that which you are able to handle. So whatever you are going through or whatever the situation is, it is for your good that God may draw you closer to Him for then we can learn what God is truly capable of doing and just how awesome He really is. Yes, being stripped hurts…Yes, it feel like you're all alone…Yes, it is frustrating and even seems unfair…But God has it under control. He is going to turn your imprisonment into a chamber of rejoicing. Whatever it takes, we must keep on doing the work that God has anointed us to do. I would not be honest if I did not say I cried many nights, yet he continued to use me and blessed others. Because no matter what I go through, I am still anointed and chosen by God to serve him and his people. In doing so, he is not going to forget my labor of love (Hebrews 6:10)…And make no mistake about it, continuing in faith, while hurting is a labor of love.

Since I am still anointed and chosen of God…since God is in control and has the enemy under His confinement…since God is faithful to complete whatever He starts…since God will cause all things to work out for in my favor, I can rest knowing that the devil is limited and there are certain things that are strictly off limits to Him. At that point, he can do no more and the situation is automatically placed right back into God's hands. It is only when I am distracted by the enemy like Eve that I relinquish my authority and risk falling. But even in that, God is still able to fix it.

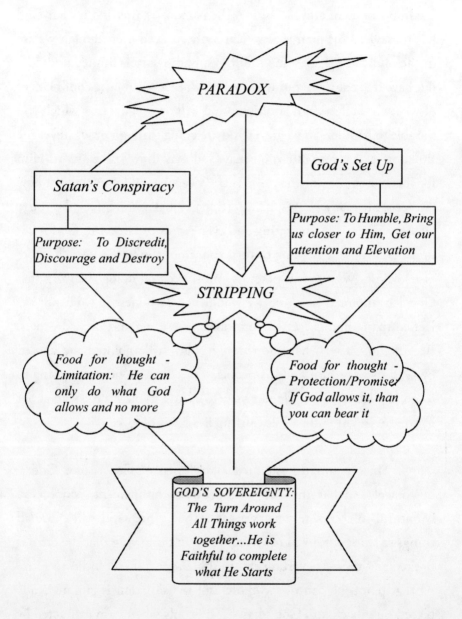

PROSPER AS MY SOUL DOES

1 John 3:2, "Beloved, I wish above all things that thou mayest prosper and be in health, even as thy soul prospereth." To prosper means to have good success. The world views success as having money and prestige. It is becoming famous and world known. But, to the Christian, good success has nothing to do with materialistic possessions. For us, excellent success only comes through Jesus Christ. It is not what we own but rather who we are. It does not settle for less than what God said you would be and would have. Your success is based on how much of the word is in you and you in Him. Whenever you think about what you want to achieve and where you want to go, begin to measure your level of obedience, submission and how much you please God. On June 25, 2004, Elder Joan Glass spoke to the 2004 graduating class of Nothing But the Word Deliverance Church Bible Institute. The theme for the commencement exercise was "Soar into Excellence." Elder Glass spoke about eagles. She stated, "Eagles like high places and live in high ground. They fly toward the sun." As David began to worship God, he began to say who God is and what he does. He writes, "Who satisfies your mouth [your necessity and desire at your personal age and situation] with good so that your youth, renewed, is like the eagle's [strong, overcoming, soaring] (Psalms 103:5-AMP)!" If we are to be like eagles, we have to live high, think high and above this world and its circumstances. Does it mean we should be conceded and puffed up. No, not at all! But it does mean we have to remember who we are and walk accordingly. Kings do not live as vagrants or derelicts. Neither should a child of God. But we can only prosper in Jesus Christ just as an unborn fetus cannot survive outside of the mother's body until such time when the child is born. For us, that will be in glory.

We have to maintain to survive. Maintaining means keep up a diligent and wise pace. It is continuing in the path you started until you reach the end. Maintaining your momentum means sticking to it regardless of what obstacles confront you and not allowing people, circumstances and situations to knock you off your intended course. Maintain your relationship with God. Imagine buying a new car. Although the car is new, the owner still has to keep up the proper maintenance so that the vehicle will continue to fulfill its purpose and meet the needs of the owner.

Joshua 1:8 (amp) reads, "This Book of the Law shall not depart out of your mouth, but you shall meditate on it day and night, that you may observe and do according to all that is written in it. For then you shall make your way prosperous, and then you shall deal wisely and have good success." The Message Version reads from verses 7-9 as follows:

> *⁷Give it everything you have, heart and soul. Make sure you carry out The Revelation that Moses commanded you, every bit of it. Don't get off track, either left or right, so as to make sure you get to where you're going. ⁸And don't for a minute let this Book of The Revelation be out of mind. Ponder and meditate on it day and night, making sure you practice everything written in it. Then you'll get where you're going; then you'll succeed. ⁹Haven't I commanded you? Strength! Courage! Don't be timid; don't get discouraged. GOD, your God, is with you every step you take."*

Is the answer that simple? Is the key to my success tied to my obedience and fellowship with Christ? Is good success contingent upon my ability to focus on my relationship with Christ and on Him only? So, by meditating on His word day and night, by holding fast to His promises and by trusting in Him enough to be obedient to Him guarantees my success! Let's add to this thought from Leviticus chapter 26, which reads:

> *"If you live by my decrees and obediently keep my commandments, 4I will send the rains in their seasons, the ground will yield its crops and the trees of the field their fruit. 5You will thresh until the grape harvest and the grape harvest will continue until planting time; you'll have more than enough to eat and will live safe and secure in your land. 6"I'll make the country a place of peace--you'll be able to go to sleep at night without fear; I'll get rid of the wild beasts; I'll eliminate war. 7You'll chase out your enemies and defeat them: 8Five of you will chase a hundred, and a hundred of you will chase ten thousand and do away with them. 9I'll give you my full attention: I'll make sure you prosper, make sure you grow in numbers, and keep my covenant with you in good working order. 10You'll still be eating from last year's harvest when you have to clean out the barns to make room for the new crops.*

Sisters, you have been wondering what it would take just to be happy again. We have been wondering if this is as good as it gets. No, its not! It took some tears, disappointments, frustration and heartbreaks for me to realize that my best is tied to my submission to the Wonderful Spirit of God. I determine my heights and depths by my ability to holdfast to His decree and to abide by His laws. The key is focusing on what is most important. The most important thing is you living up to your design.

WHILE HE IS WORKING ON YOU, REMEMBER THIS:

Proverbs 31:30-31(NKJV)

> *"Charm it deceitful, and beauty is passing, but a woman who fears the Lord, she shall be praised. Give her of the fruit of her hands; and let her own works praise her in the gates."*

1 Peter 3:3-4(NKJV)

> *"Do not let you adornment be merely outward - arranging the hair, wearing gold, or putting on fine apparel - rather let it be the hidden person of the heart, with the incorruptible beauty of a gentle and quiet spirit, which is very precious in the sight of God.*

While you are being tested and tried, remember this:

Isaiah 59:19 (KJV)

> *" So shall they fear the name of the Lord from the west, and his glory from the rising of the sun. When the enemy shall come in like a flood, the Spirit of the Lord shall lift up a standard against him."*

2 Chronicles 20:15b(NKJV)

> *"...For the battle is not yours, but God's."*

WHEN YOU FEEL LIKE GIVING UP, REMEMBER THIS:

Hebrews 3:14 (NKJV)

"For we have become partakers of Christ if we hold the beginning of our confidence steadfast to the end."

1 Corinthians 15:58 (KJV)

"Therefore, my beloved brethren, be ye stedfast, unmoveable, always abounding in the work of the Lord, forasmuch as ye know that your labour is not in vain in the Lord."

WHEN IT SEEMS LIKE GOD IS TAKING TO LONG, REMEMBER THIS:

Psalms 27:14(KJV)

"Wait on the Lord; be of good courage, and He shall strengthen thine heart."

Proverbs 20:22b(KJV)

"...Wait on the Lord, and he shall save thee."

FINALLY, WHEN YOU FEEL LIKE GOD DOES NOT HEAR YOUR CRIES, REMEMBER THIS:

Deuteronomy 31:8(NKJV)

"And the Lord, He is the One who goes before you. He will be with you, He will not leave you nor forsake you; do not fear nor be dismayed."

Romans 8:28(KJV)

"And we know that all things work together for good to them that love God, to them who are the called according to his purpose."

REFLECTION

1. What do you think about your singleness?

2. How do you see yourself?

3. What or who are you still holding on to?

4. Have you truly forgiven your offender?

5. What would you ask God to change right now?

6. Are you in relationships that have become a hindrance?

7. Name three areas in your life you want to change that will better your Christian walk.

8. Evaluate your level of faith. Have you been a negative tool?

9. Rank your level of consistency.

10. What do you feel is the area in your life, which lacks in consistency?

11. What can you do to change that?

12. What are you going to do now?

13. What are you going to do with all the power and gifts God has given you?

14. What will you do to prepare yourself for this war that we are engaged in?

15. What will it take for you to get to your next level?

16. What can you do in your church and for your Pastor that will add to the ministry?

17. What contributions can you make that will add to Kingdom Building?

ENDNOTES

1. www.apostolic-churches.net/bible/strongs.html

2 . www.webmd.com – article "Genetics of Coronary Heart Disease"

4. www.mayoclinic.com – article "Coronary Artery Disease"

5. www.bsu.edu – article "Comparing Tree Rings"

6. users.aber.ac.uk – article "Introduction of Dendrochronology"

7. *Webster's New World Dictionary* 3rd Edition

8. Reverend Milton Brunson "Available to You" 1988

9. *Webster's New World Dictionary* 3rd Edition

10. www.apostolic-churches.net/bible/strongs

11. Pastor Harry Morgan. NBTWDC 1st Singles Service. February 19, 2005. Florence, New Jersey.

12. Hagin, Kenneth. *Believer's Authority.* 1986. Rhema Bible Church. Tulsa, Oklahoma.

13. Pastor Allyn Waller. "Love – 1 Corinthians 13." April 27, 2004. Philadelphia, Pennsylvania.

14. www.apostolic-churches.net/bible/strongs.html

15. Vine, W.E. *Vine's Complete Expository Dictionary.* 1996. Thomas Nelson, Inc. Nashville, TN.

14. *Webster's New World Dictionary:* Third College Edition

15. John Hopkins Medicine "Broken Heart Syndrome: Real, Potentially Deadly but Recovery Quick" Febraty 9, 2005

16. www.apostolic-churches.net/bible/strongs

17. Donald Lawrence & The Tri-City Singers "Go Get Your Life Back"

ABOUT THE AUTHOR

Minister Tara A. Black was born in Willingboro, New Jersey in 1972, where she graduated from Willingboro High School in 1990. Upon graduation, she attended Rutgers University acquiring a Bachelor's in Social Work. Minister Black has also received her Masters in Business Administration from Eastern University, a designation of Professional, Academy of Healthcare (PAHM) and is currently enrolled in the Bible Institute of N.B.T.W.D.C. She has been employed by Independence Blue Cross since September, 1994 where she is currently a Manager of Physician Reimbursement.

Being called to the ministry at a young age, Minister Black began preaching at the age of 16 under the pastorate of Apostle Eric F. Ricks of Faith Deliverance Worship Center, formerly called Deliverance Evangelistic Church, in Burlington, New Jersey. Under his leadership, she served the ministry as an usher, choir directress, youth leader and an aspiring minister. Minister Black was also a member of Christ Community Evangelistic Church of Willingboro, NJ where she served on the ministerial staff and as Minister of Music.

As Minister Black continues to grow in the Lord, she found a new home under the ministry of Rev. Dr. Patricia A. Phillips, pastor and founder of Nothing but the Word Deliverance Church in Florence,

New Jersey. There she proudly serves as a minister, assistant director of the women's ministry, worship coordinator and director of the women's choir. Minister Black began to expand her ministry by writing a book called Waiting on Your Promise, which was written to encourage single women everywhere and is in the process of being published. In addition, she continues to carry a burden for unwed mothers and has already begun the inception a second book designed for this burden titled All on Her Own: A Mother's Spiritual Cookbook.

All of her accomplishments, including being nominated for Who's Who among High School Students, are a result of what a Great God she serves. There is no other explanation, except God has the final say over her life. As a result of his blessings and her love for the Lord, Minister Black faithfully serves as a counselor, mentor, teacher, writer and preacher. In addition, she recognizes her responsibility to her family and her loving son, Tyree' Black. Minister Black's ability to be the best mother she can is most important to her, providing him with a firm foundation and example through the Word of God and hard work.

Printed in the United States
83419LV00007B/111/A

9 781420 895322